D0615527

TERRORISM

WITHDRAWN

**REVISED
EDITION**

TERRORISM

PAST, PRESENT,
FUTURE

**BY THOMAS
RAYNOR**

Franklin Watts / 1987
New York / London / Toronto / Sydney

"Easter 1916" is reprinted with permission of
Macmillan Publishing Co., Inc. from
Collected Poems of William Butler Yeats.
Copyright 1924 by Macmillan Publishing Co., Inc.,
renewed 1952 by Bertha Georgie Yeats.

Library of Congress Cataloging-in-Publication Data

Raynor, Thomas P.
Terrorism : past, present, future.

Bibliography: p.
Includes index.
Summary: Discusses various forms of terrorism from
the execution of Marie Antoinette in the late
eighteenth century to the increasingly serious problem
that terrorism poses for the entire world community
today.
1. Terrorism—History—Juvenile literature.
[1. Terrorism—History]   I. Title.
HV6431.R39   1987   303.6'25'09   86-28074
ISBN 0-531-10344-7

Copyright © 1987 by Thomas Raynor
All rights reserved
Printed in the United States of America
6   5   4   3   2

CONTENTS

TERRORISM

PART I

THE BEGINNINGS

CHAPTER ONE

FACES OF
TERRORISM

If the mainspring of popular government in time of peace is virtue, the mainspring of popular government in time of revolution is both virtue and terror. Without virtue, terror is evil; without terror, virtue is helpless.

*Maximilien Robespierre,
in a speech before
the National Convention,
Paris, 1794*

From *The Times* of London, October 23, 1793, comes an account of one of the very first acts of terrorism. The report appears under the headline, "Execution of the Queen of France":

PARIS, Oct. 22. It is with sincere regret we confirm the general report of yesterday, respecting the fate of this unfortunate princess, who suffered under the axe of the guillotine on Wednesday last the 16th instant; after having been condemned on the preceding day by the National Convention as guilty of having . . . cooperated in different manoeuvres against the liberty of France.

The execution took place at half past eleven o'clock in the forenoon. The whole armed force in Paris was on foot, from the Palace of Justice to the Place de la Revolution. The streets were lined by two very close rows of armed citizens.

As soon as the former Queen left the [prison], to ascend to the scaffold, the multitude which was assembled in the courts and the streets, cried out "Bravo!" in the midst of plaudits. Marie Antoinette had on a white loose dress, and her hands were tied behind her on all sides. She was accompanied by the former Curate of St. Landry, a constitutional priest, and on the scaffold preserved her natural dignity of mind.

After the execution three young persons dipped their handkerchiefs in her blood. They were immediately arrested.

[13]

A SYSTEM
OF VIOLENCE

In her prison in Paris, Marie Antoinette had been relatively harmless. No meaningful treason justified her execution. But her death would serve as a warning to others. It was an important element in the strategy of violence through which Maximilien Robespierre and a small faction of the Jacobin party dominated France for a period in 1793–94. They were the first to use violence systematically—as a method of suppressing opposition and enhancing their own power. For this reason, Robespierre's rule has come to be known as "the Reign of Terror." From that period have come the French and English words *terrorisme* and terrorism. And since 1798, when it first appeared in a dictionary, the word terrorism has implied the systematic use of violence to achieve political objectives.

The success of terrorism depends on the fear it creates. By killing, or threatening to kill, members of every class or group —by killing even the Queen—Robespierre convinced twenty-seven million citizens of France that none of them was secure. Fear paralyzed all potential opposition—for a while. The executions and all the other acts of violence were aimed not so much at the victims, as at those who watched. And because fear is essential to the success of terrorism, so is publicity. If an act of terrorism fails to attract attention, then it fails to frighten people. Well aware of this point, Robespierre made a spectacle of the beheading of Marie Antoinette. In all respects, he pioneered what is called "state terrorism."

THE SHADOW
OF ROBESPIERRE

State terrorism is more common today than it was in the time of Robespierre. Since the 1960s the techniques of state terrorism have been refined, and it has posed an increasingly serious problem for the entire world community. Evidence of major —and continuing—state terrorism was revealed in a *New York Times* story that appeared on September 22, 1976, bearing the headline, "Opponent of Chilean Junta Slain in Washington by Bomb in His Auto":

WASHINGTON, Sept. 21. Orlando Letelier, who was foreign minister in the Chilean government of President

Salvador Allende Gossens, was killed here today when a bomb exploded in his car as it sped along fashionable Embassy Row. . . . Mr. Letelier was a leader of Chilean political exiles in this country who opposed the military junta that overthrew President Allende in 1973. . . .

Mr. Letelier, who was 44 years old, had told acquaintances that he feared for his life immediately after release from nearly a year of imprisonment in the junta's prisons two years ago. During a brief stay in 1974 in Venezuela, he told a *New York Times* reporter, "They're going to kill me," and then mentioned the "DINA," an acronym for the Spanish name for the secret police. . . . [An] associate, who asked not to be identified, said that United States authorities had informed Mr. Letelier last May that some DINA agents were thought to be circulating in this country.

The associate also recalled that Mr. Letelier had made his "last public speech" on Sept. 19 at a rally in the Felt Forum of Madison Square Garden, where he commented on his deprivation of citizenship. On that occasion he said: "I was born a Chilean, I am a Chilean, and I will die a Chilean. They, the fascists, were born traitors, live as traitors and will be remembered forever as fascist traitors."

TERRORISM
GOES INTERNATIONAL

United States prosecutors believe that Letelier's death was ordered by the DINA. The man who admits to planting the fatal bomb claims that he was acting for the DINA. Three high officials of the DINA were indicted in the U.S. but could not be extradited. DINA was also linked to the 1974 murder of a Chilean general and his wife in Argentina, and to the 1975 gun attack on the founder of Chile's Christian Democratic party and his wife in Rome. In other words, Letelier's murder was part of the systematic violence by which Chile's junta rules.

Other elements in the Chilean system of violence, as documented by Amnesty International and other observers, have been more than five thousand executions, the arbitrary arrest and detainment of more than one hundred thousand persons, the forced exile of tens of thousands, and many thousands of "disappearances." Although the junta's methods differ from Robespierre's, its purpose is the same: to create fear that will paralyze all the opponents of unpopular government and anti-democratic rule.

DINA terrorism is state terrorism that has gone international. Once, it was assumed that terrorism was a domestic problem: Russian terrorists operated in Russia; Irish terrorists, in Ireland, and so on. But since the 1960s, terrorism has become increasingly international in its scope, with Japanese terrorists operating in the Middle East; Palestinians, in Europe and Latin America; and Chileans, in the United States.

REVOLUTIONARY
TERRORISM
So far the subject has been state terrorism. Not for a century after the Reign of Terror—not until the 1870s—did revolutionaries adopt terrorism as a method of attacking a government. An account of one of the first and most important acts of revolutionary terrorism was published in the *New York Times* on February 6, 1878, under the headline, "Attempt by a Woman to Shoot the Prefect of St. Petersburg":

ST. PETERSBURG, Feb. 5. While M. Trepov, Prefect [military governor] of St. Petersburg was giving today the usual audience for the reception of petitions, a woman fired upon him twice with a revolver. The Prefect was dangerously wounded by one of the shots; the ball has not been extracted. The Emperor and Prince Gortschakoff have visited him. The city is greatly excited. The woman, who was immediately arrested, preserves complete silence in regard to her motives.

Eventually the *Times* reporter discovered the would-be assassin's name. She was Vera Zasulich, the twenty-nine-year-old daughter of a nobleman. Because she had no motive other than to rid Russia of a tyrant, her trial became an indictment of the tsarist regime.

Surprisingly, she was acquitted and released. She was ordered rearrested, but escaped. Years later she returned to the Soviet Union, becoming a legend in the Soviet revolutionary pantheon. Her attempt on General Trepov's life was the catalyst for the formation of the first revolutionary terrorist group, the People's Will.

In a later edition, the *Times* reported that the assassination attempt "was said to have made a deep impression on the mind of the tsar, and to have filled him with gloomy forebodings that he himself may be murdered." His forebodings proved to be justified. Monarchs had been assassinated in the past, but Tsar Alexander II was the first to fall prey to revolutionary terrorists.

Revolutionary terrorism has become more commonplace in our time than it was when the People's Will operated. Terrorists dedicated to the destruction of the existing government have been active in the United States, West Germany, Italy, the Middle East, and elsewhere. And like state terrorists, revolutionary terrorists have gone international, striking "soft" targets anywhere in the world virtually at will.

NATIONALISM
AND TERRORISM
In addition to state terrorism and revolutionary terrorism, there is the terrorism of the militant nationalist who demands separation from another country—Ireland from England or Algeria from France, for example. "Nationalist-separatist" terrorism, as this form of terrorism is known, has been a potent force throughout the history of terrorism.

From the *New York Times*, July 23, 1946, comes this account of an act of nationalist-separatist terrorism committed by the Jewish Palestinian Irgun under the headline, "Jerusalem Bomb Kills 41 in Attack on British Offices":

JERUSALEM, July 22. An entire six-story corner and basement at the southwestern wing of the King David Hotel were destroyed and at least forty-one British, Jewish and Arab Government officials were killed and fifty-three were injured soon after midday when terrorists believed to belong to either Irgun Zvai Leumi or the Stern gang, blew up a large part of the offices of the chief secretary of the Palestine Government. . . .

[17]

[The explosion] was preceded by a mysterious telephone warning to the hotel's switchboard operator by a woman caller who said: "Tell everyone to leave the hotel. It is going to be blown up in a few minutes."

An eyewitness, Maj. Eric Merrill, army public-relations officer, who was in the building opposite the hotel, told me: "First there was a great explosion. Then the southwestern corner of the hotel seemed to bulge. It collapsed with a great roar and a huge column of brown-gray smoke billowed up."

Men and women staggered from the hotel, dazed from shock, their faces covered with white dust and many streaked with blood from head wounds. Others, unable to walk, were being helped. Government employees, British military men, messenger boys and hotel guests came out in a long stream. A passing bus was blown off course and every passenger was injured.

The Irgun's bombing of the King David Hotel was in line with its policy of attacking British property interests in Palestine. The Irgun insists that it gave the British ample time to evacuate the building—twenty-two minutes. Yet the death toll reached ninety-one, and the death of innocents deprived the Irgun of the justification that their terrorism was "selective"—that is, aimed only at the "oppressor." The incident provides a good example of how "selective" terrorism often slides unintentionally into random terrorism.

OTHER FORMS
OF TERRORISM

Other forms of terrorism stem from racist or religious motives. One such act of terrorism was described in the *New York Times* on March 26, 1965, under the headline, "Woman Is Shot to Death on Lowndes County Road":

MONTGOMERY, ALA., March 25. A white woman worker for the Southern Christian Leadership Conference was shot to death tonight while returning to Montgomery from Selma, Ala., where she had delivered a carload of civil rights workers who took part in the Freedom March that ended here today.

The woman, Mrs. Viola Gregg Liuzzo, 38 years old, was a member of the transportation committee of the civil rights march and was completing her third day as a transport driver.

She was shot on U.S. Highway 80 a mile from Lowndesboro in Lowndes County. The small village is about half way between Selma and Montgomery. The only witness to the slaying was a Negro youth, Leroy Moten, about 17, who was in the front seat of the 1963 sedan that Mrs. Liuzzo was driving.

Mr. Moten said Mrs. Liuzzo had been shot through the head or neck by a high-powered rifle . . . by a group of unidentified men in another car. . . . Mrs. Liuzzo lost control of her car when she was shot and it traveled several hundred feet along the shoulder of the road before it stopped. . . .

On the day following Mrs. Liuzzo's death, President Lyndon B. Johnson announced the arrest of four members of the Ku Klux Klan in connection with the slaying. In a dramatic television appearance, the president declared "war" on the Klan, saying: "I shall continue to fight them because I know their loyalty is not to the United States of America but instead to a hooded society of bigotry." That same day, the Imperial Wizard of the United Klans of America called the president a "damn liar."

Despite condemnation, the Klan survives—and thrives. Founded in 1867, it is one of the oldest terrorist groups in the world. Unlike other terrorists, Klansmen rarely take credit for their violence, recognizing perhaps that they could lose more sympathy than they might attract; recognizing, too, that fear is the real object. Klan-created fear played an important part in sabotaging the post–Civil War reconstruction that Abraham Lincoln desired and preserving white supremacy in the South. Klan violence qualifies as terrorism because it is systematic, and because its objective is basically political—the preservation by one group of its power over another.

Terrorists can have religious as well as racist motives. The assassins of President Anwar Sadat of Egypt in 1981 were members of a group of Moslem terrorists called Atonement and Repentance. Using systematic violence, they aim to overthrow the Egyptian state and create an Islamic Republic like that created by the Ayatollah Ruhollah Khomeini in Iran. Throughout the Middle East, among Arabs and non-Arabs alike, incidents of terrorism by religious fundamentalists are on the rise.

TERRORISTS, CRIMINALS, AND GUERRILLAS

Terrorism can take the form of almost any crime—murder, kidnapping, robbery, or arson, for example. But terrorism differs from ordinary criminal violence in two ways. First, the terrorist's purpose—unlike that of the criminal—is psychological. When a mugger attacks a victim, his objective is money. When terrorists attack, they seek to frighten others and to publicize their cause. Although it is true that a crime wave can "terrorize" a community, fear is the unintended by-product of crime. But it is the terrorist's basic objective.

Second, the objectives of terrorism, unlike those of crime, are political. The long-term, or strategic, objectives of terrorism—as illustrated in the examples above—include the repression of dissent, revolution, and national liberation. The short-term, or tactical, objectives of terrorism include freeing captured comrades, obtaining ransoms, seizing arms and ammunition, embarrassing the authorities, and forcing people to choose sides between the terrorists and the government.

Terrorism also differs from guerrilla warfare, even though terrorists sometimes refer to themselves as "urban guerrillas." Guerrillas are members of irregular armies that fight a government in the countryside, developing popular support as they do so. Eventually, as guerrilla leader and theorist Mao Zedong said, "the countryside envelops the cities" and the government is overthrown. In contrast with guerrillas, terrorists operate mainly in the cities, and have never been successful in mobilizing popular support. For that reason, terrorist groups are often described as "elitist," as opposed to "popular," movements.

LESSONS OF TERRORISM

As documented in the cases and episodes that follow, the history of terrorism offers practical lessons. Terrorism has been practiced by governments against their citizens, and by citizens against their governments. It has been practiced by militants on the left, as well as on the right.

Terrorism occurs frequently in societies we call "democratic," but rarely in communist or fascist societies. It can be totally eliminated, but only at the cost of democratic and constitutional values.

History further reveals that terrorism has rarely been successful in achieving its promised strategic objectives—revolution or national independence, for example—and that techniques of nonviolent resistance have scored more striking victories. Nevertheless, as headlines daily reveal, the destructive fascination of the terrorist persists.

CHAPTER
TWO

TERRORISM
AND
REVOLUTION

The revolutionary despises all political programs, and has rejected the ordinary sciences, leaving them to future generations. He knows only one science—that of destruction. . . . His sole, unswerving objective is the total destruction of this vile system.

Sergey Nechaev,
Catechism of the
Revolutionary, *1869*

From the French Revolution of 1789–99 have come some of our most basic political concepts and much of our political vocabulary. Before the French Revolution, the word "revolution" meant simply the changing fortunes of government. But ever since the French middle class overthrew the aristocracy in 1789, "revolution" has meant a basic reversal of the relationship between social classes.

It was the philosophers of the French Enlightenment who had opened the door to revolution by questioning the divine right of kings. And it was the French philosophers, especially Jean-Jacques Rousseau, who gave us the modern notion of nationalism. Rousseau rejected the idea that a nation was personified in the monarch or aristocracy. Instead, said Rousseau, the nation is the people. This was a subversive idea, especially to great empires such as Austria-Hungary. It implied that all of the empire's many peoples—Hungarians, Czechs, Serbians, and others—were entitled to nationhood. And indeed, each of those peoples soon demanded independence.

There was no kingdom or empire in Europe that was not threatened by the ideas of revolution and nationalism, and by the values expressed in the French revolutionary slogan, "Liberty, Equality, Fraternity." As early as 1793, the Venetian ambassador in Vienna warned his government:

> The arms of the French are all the more dangerous since the poison of their thought is diffused everywhere, and by preceding their armies contributes to their suc-

cess. . . . The people imagine that their poverty will be relieved by such doctrines. . . .

It is above all worthy of remark, how even the lowest class of the people . . . now turn their attention to the present war, and reason in their own way about the motives that have brought it on. . . .

The French Revolution is gradually bringing another equally dangerous revolution in the universal way of thinking

THE REIGN OF TERROR

The basic vocabulary of politics emerged from the French Revolution. The term "left" and "right" come from the French practice of seating radicals and liberals on the left side of the legislative chamber, as viewed from the president's chair, and the reactionaries and conservatives on the right. In the original French chamber, the "leftists" favored continued change aimed at creating a greater degree of social equality. "Rightists" wanted to go more slowly—either to consolidate the change that had already taken place, or to resist change altogether. Leftists preferred a participatory—or democratic—form of government, whereas rightists preferred a representative—or republican—form of government, or a monarchy.

From the French left came the Jacobin party and its leader Maximilien Robespierre, who wanted to create a "moral republic" in which higher values would be not merely emphasized, but enforced: "We desire morality instead of selfishness; honesty and not mere 'honor'; principle and not mere custom; duty and not mere respectability; the sway of reason rather than the tyranny of fashion."

Intolerant of those who opposed the idea of a "moral republic," Robespierre declared them "enemies of the people" to whom the government owed "nothing but death." Violence and threats of violence were justified in dealing with opponents, he argued, because France was at war. Thus terrorism was consciously adopted as a method of rule. "Terror," said Robespierre, "is nothing but justice—prompt, severe, and inflexible. It is therefore the release of virtue."

Those who criticize the "moral republic" were declared traitors. Anyone and everyone became vulnerable to charges of treason. And Robespierre's suspicions were sufficient grounds for the conviction and execution of personal and political enemies. Altogether, some seventeen thousand persons perished, including peasants, workers, and aristocrats. By the summer of 1794 the opposition was paralyzed with fear. All powers had become centralized in the Paris government, including the power to define virtue. And virtue came to mean nothing more than harmlessness to the government.

In July 1794 Robespierre revealed to the delegates of the National Convention that he possessed a list of "traitors" in their midst, although he would not reveal the names on the list. This was a tactic he had used in the past to stifle opposition. But this time the tactic proved to be Robespierre's undoing. By now his opposition was strong enough, and sufficiently threatened, to unite against him. By an act of the National Convention, Robespierre was deposed and he and his collaborators were executed.

Robespierre's Reign of Terror is the first example of state terrorism in history. Robespierre showed the world how violence and threats of violence could be used systematically by governments to intimidate their opponents and enhance their power. In the century that followed, Russian dissidents would show the world how terrorism could be used against governments by those intent on revolution.

A REVOLUTIONARY
SITUATION
Among those who were influenced by revolutionary events in eighteenth- and nineteenth-century France was Karl Marx, the founder of a form of socialism known variously as Marxism, Marxism-Leninism, and communism. Marx and others often described Russia as "the France of the nineteenth century." And contemporary historians agree that there were important parallels between the two societies. In *The Age of the Democratic Revolution*, historian R. R. Palmer describes the "revolutionary situation" that existed in both eighteenth-century France and nineteenth-century Russia:

By a revolutionary situation is here meant one in which confidence in the justice or reasonableness of existing

[27]

authority is undermined; where old loyalties fade, obligations are felt as impositions, law seems arbitrary, and respect for superiors is felt as a form of humiliation; where existing sources of wealth and income seem ill gained, and government is sensed as distant, apart from the governed and not really "representing" them. In such a situation the sense of community is lost, and the bond between social classes turns to jealousy and frustration. . . . Something must happen, if continuing deterioration is to be avoided; some new kind or basis of community must be formed.

A revolutionary situation had been developing in Russia for more than a century. In the 1600s and the 1700s, there had been great peasant revolts, all of them ruthlessly suppressed by the tsar's government. In 1861 the government emancipated the peasants, raising hopes for democratic reforms. But the reforms never materialized. The peasants remained socially oppressed; the reformers became bitterly disappointed; and public opinion of the government and its policies worsened by the year.

What Marx and his followers foresaw in Russia was a revolution by the middle class, such as France had experienced. Then, according to Marx's theory of revolution, after the capitalists had created an industrial society and a working class, the workers would overthrow the middle class and create a socialist state. But the workers' revolution and socialism lay in the distant future in Russia, Marx believed, and he was far more interested in the prospects for workers' revolutions in France, Germany, and England.

Marx observed the Russian situation from afar: from London, where he and his collaborator, Friedrich Engels, lived and worked. And even though Marxists led by V. I. Lenin would one day seize power in Russia, they were a small minority among Russian socialists and revolutionaries in the 1870s. Far more numerous and influential than the Marxists during these years were the Populists.

The Populists were socialists who believed that the peasants, not the workers, would launch the revolution in Russia. In the mid-1870s the Populists organized a massive "movement to the people," going to the countryside, living among the peasants, sharing their burdens, and propagandizing them, hoping to release their revolutionary fervor. The movement peaked in the summer of 1874, when thousands of Populists went to the people. Because most of them were students, the Populists seemed "suspicious" to the peasants, who turned many of them over to the police. Hundreds of them were sentenced to prison or exile, thus ending the movement. The tsarist regime, the most despotic and repressive system in Europe, remained untouched.

VOICES OF TERRORISM

The Marxists and the Russian Populists believed that a revolutionary situation required time to mature—that revolution would come only when conditions were ripe. Others argued that bold and violent acts could ignite a revolution at any time, as long as a revolutionary situation existed. These others were the first revolutionary terrorists. For the Populists' "propaganda of the word," the terrorists proposed to substitute "propaganda of the deed"—assassinations and bombings that would paralyze the government and lead the masses to revolt. Two of the earliest voices of revolutionary terrorism were Mikhail Bakunin and Sergey Nechaev.

Born in 1814, Bakunin was the son of landed gentry. He was educated in a military school in St. Petersburg and served as an officer in the privileged guards. At twenty, he resigned his commission, unwilling to serve the repressive tsarist system. He went to Moscow, where he worked as a free-lance journalist, preaching revolution and making contact with other would-be revolutionaries. His activities in Moscow marked him as a dangerous suspect in the eyes of the tsarist secret police, and in 1840 he left Russia for the West. He took an active part in the wave of revolutions that swept Europe in 1848 and 1849, fighting on the side of rebels in France, Austria, and Germany.

In 1849 Bakunin was arrested by the Austrian police and handed over to the Russian government. In Russia he was charged with revolutionary activities, tried, convicted, and sentenced to life imprisonment. He had served six years of his sentence when it was commuted to a lifetime exile in Siberia. From Siberia, in 1861, Bakunin made a sensational escape aboard an American ship bound for Japan. From Japan, he made his way to the United States and then to Europe, where he preached and practiced revolution in France, Italy, and Poland.

Like Marx, Bakunin believed that violent revolution was necessary to overthrow capitalism and establish socialism. Beyond that, the two agreed on nothing. Bakunin was vehemently opposed to the existence of government, which he saw as the source of all social evils. He denounced Marx for wanting to smash the capitalist state only to replace it with a socialist state. In Bakunin's vision of socialism, which is called anarchism, even "the smallest and most inoffensive state is still criminal."

Bakunin and the anarchists glorified violence. "The urge to destroy," wrote Bakunin, "is also a creative urge." He sanctioned every form of violence: "We recognize no other action but destruction, though we admit that the form in which such action will show itself will be exceedingly varied: poison, the knife, the noose and so on. Everything in this fight is equally sanctified by the revolution." Unlike Marx, Bakunin had no faith in the workers, who he believed could be bought off with crumbs. Instead he placed his hopes for revolution in the destructive instincts of the peasants, who would be led by criminals and radical intellectuals such as himself.

Bakunin developed a justification for terrorism against the state that would surface in our own time. The state, he argued, is more guilty than the terrorist who attacks it:

> It is considerably more humane to stab and strangle dozens, even hundreds, of hated human beings than to join with them to share in systematic *legal* acts of murder, in the torture and martyrdom of millions of peasants. . . . All healthy young minds [should] commit themselves to the *sacred cause* of rooting out evil, purifying and cleansing Russia's soil by fire and sword. . . .

In 1872 Bakunin and his followers were expelled from the Socialist International, a worldwide organization of socialist parties dominated by Marx and his followers. In arguing for

Bakunin's expulsion, Marx explicitly denounced Bakunin's advocacy of terrorism, even though Marx himself had occasionally applauded a terrorist act. Basically, argued Marx and Engels, revolutions are made by social classes, not by a few conspirators. Disgraced in the eyes of the world's socialists, Bakunin died in 1876. Even so, his influence survived him. He had expressed an argument for terrorism that has seduced even Marxists and attracts followers even today.

"THE POSSESSED"

Sergey Nechaev was born in 1847. His father—first a house painter, then a builder—was a member of Russia's small middle class. Rather than follow in his father's footsteps, Sergey decided to enter a university. He arrived in St. Petersburg when he was twenty-one years old and immediately became active in conspiratorial circles. Within several months of his arrival in the capital, he was in charge of a broad network of revolutionary groups. He would dominate the Russian revolutionary scene even from his dungeon.

In late 1869 a fellow student was killed on Nechaev's orders. As a result, Nechaev had to flee to Western Europe, where he met and worked with Bakunin. In 1872 Nechaev was arrested by the Swiss police and handed over to the tsarist police as a common criminal. In 1873 he was tried for his role in the student's murder. Convicted, he received a twenty-year prison sentence.

Two important documents owe their origin to Nechaev: Dostoevsky's novel *The Possessed*, which is based on the story of Nechaev and his circle of revolutionary terrorists, and Nechaev's own *Catechism of the Revolutionary*, in which Bakunin had a hand. Like Bakunin, Nechaev glorified violence. "Our task," he wrote, "is terrible, total, universal and merciless destruction." Through terrorism, Nechaev believed, the revolutionary could rally all those isolated individuals who opposed the existing regime and deprive those who supported it of their peace and comfort. And only through terrorism, he wrote, could the revolutionary achieve his long-term, strategic objective: "to destroy every object root and branch, to annihilate all state traditions, orders and classes."

Nechaev developed the organizational structure of a terrorist

[31]

group that serves as a model for terrorists today. In Nechaev's structure, terrorists are organized in small groups, or cells. Two members of each cell also belong to other cells, serving as coordinators. Thus three cells are linked, but only two persons are familiar with the membership and plans of more than one cell. By organizing themselves as Nechaev suggested, terrorists reduce the risk of police infiltration, as well as the possibility that a captured member might reveal too much information under torture.

IN THE SHADOW
OF NECHAEV

Virtually all terrorist groups—from the Irish Republican Army to the Black Panthers—have used Nechaev's organizational principles, or some variation of them. And even though V. I. Lenin, the leader of Russia's Marxists and founder of the Soviet state, was generally opposed to terrorism, he was influenced by Nechaev in organizing his Bolshevik party. Of Nechaev, Lenin wrote: "He possessed unique organizational talent, an ability to establish the special techniques of conspiratorial work everywhere, an ability to give his thoughts such startling formulations that they were forever imprinted on one's memory."

Nechaev's characterization of the revolutionary terrorist may have been one of the "startling formulations" that so impressed Lenin, whose younger brother was executed as a terrorist:

> The revolutionary is a doomed man. He has no interests of his own, no feelings, no attachments, no belongings, no name. Everything in him is subordinated to a single exclusive aim, a single thought, a single passion: the revolution. He is an implacable enemy of this world, and if he continues to live in it, that will be only to destroy it more effectively. . . .
>
> He despises the existing social ethic in all its demands and expressions. For him, everything that allows the triumph of the revolution is moral. . . . The revolutionary passion which in him becomes a habitual state of mind must at each moment be combined with cold calculation. . . . He must be ready to destroy himself

and destroy with his own hands everyone who stands in his way.

If Lenin was impressed, so were others. In the 1970s Black Panther Eldridge Cleaver would write: "I took *The Catechism* for my bible and consciously began to incorporate these principles into my daily life." But Nechaev's ideas would bear fruit in his own lifetime.

THE PEOPLE'S WILL

The Populists' "movement to the people" had failed in 1874. At the same time, the ideas of Bakunin and Nechaev circulated more and more freely. The trend toward terrorism was intensified in 1878 by the attempted assassination of General F. F. Trepov, military governor of St. Petersburg, by Vera Zasulich. In 1879 the revolutionary terrorist group called the People's Will was formed. Over the next three years, its members included as few as fifty activists, and perhaps as many as five hundred. During that period, the People's Will became the fullest expression of the theory and practice of revolutionary terrorism.

Members of the People's Will acknowledged the moral dilemmas associated with the use of terrorism. They argued that they had been forced to practice terrorism because the government had closed off the possibility of peaceful reform. They promised to abandon terrorism if they saw signs of "even the possibility of an honest government." Until such time, they would act in behalf of the people, whose will they assumed they expressed.

According to the official program of the People's Will, its objectives were these:

> . . . To liquidate the worst officials, to compromise the prestige of the government, to give constant proof that it is possible to fight the government, to strengthen thereby the revolutionary spirit of the people and their faith in the cause, and finally, to form capable cadres trained in the struggle. . . .

At its first formal meeting in August 1879, the People's Will passed a solemn resolution to kill the tsar. There exists evi-

[33]

dence that its members considered and rejected an alternate action—freeing Nechaev from prison. In the Russian police archives there is a coded letter from Nechaev to the leaders of the People's Will in which he says: "Forget about me for a time and go about your own affairs. I shall watch from afar with the keenest interest." Far from remaining aloof, however, the imprisoned Nechaev was an active participant in the campaign to kill the tsar.

THE CLASSICAL CAMPAIGN

In charge of hunting the tsar were Andrei Zhelyabov, the twenty-nine-year-old son of a peasant, and Sophia Perovskaya, a twenty-six-year-old daughter of a minor nobleman. Their first plan was to mine the tsar's train as he traveled from the south of Russia to Moscow. One mining operation had already begun when the tsar changed his itinerary, and the operation was abandoned. Digging in the mud in miserably cold weather, a second team of terrorists planted dynamite under the rails of the tsar's new route. As the imperial train roared down the line, the terrorists closed the circuit with precision timing. But the charge failed to detonate. A third mine waited at the end of a 150-foot tunnel that the conspirators had dug under the tracks on which the tsar's train would enter Moscow. This time the mine exploded directly under the train. But this time, the tsar's train had preceded the train carrying his retinue, and the wrong train was destroyed.

The next move by the People's Will came in February 1880. One of the terrorists, Stepan Khalturin, was hired as a carpenter in the Winter Palace in St. Petersburg. Over a period of months, he had smuggled enough dynamite into the palace to assemble a one-hundred-pound bomb. On February 5, at about 6:15 P.M., he lit the long fuse attached to the chestful of dynamite he had placed in the basement under the imperial dining room, the Yellow Hall. The tsar, his family, and their guests were scheduled to enter the dining room at 6:30 P.M. Khalturin waited a short distance from the palace as the bomb exploded—at precisely 6:30. Eleven persons were killed and fifty-six wounded, but the tsar had been delayed and once again was spared.

Undaunted by their string of failures, the People's Will

next focused on the tsar's routes within the capital. Pretending to be merchants, two of the terrorists rented a shop on a street frequently traveled by the tsar. From one room of the shop, they dug a tunnel to the middle of the street. When ready, the tunnel would hold the dynamite to be detonated under the tsar's carriage or sled.

The target date for the assassination attempt was March 13, 1881. But suddenly, on February 27, the attempt seemed doomed. Andrey Zhelyabov was seized in a raid on the lodgings of another revolutionary. When captured, he was carrying letters the People's Will had received from Nechaev, as well as notes and codes. Now the terrorists were under extraordinary pressure to strike before the police could trace them. Replacing Zhelyabov as leader of the operation, Sofia Perovskaya moved up the date of the attempt to March 1—just two days away.

THE ATTACK
On Sunday, March 1, Alexander II was in good spirits. The news of Zhelyabov's arrest was encouraging, for it suggested that the conspiracy had been broken. The tsar went ahead with plans to attend a military review with his brother, the Grand Duke Michael, agreeing to change his usual route to avoid the street with the suspicious shop on it. Foreseeing that the route might be changed, Perovskaya had already taken the precaution of stationing four bomb-throwers along alternate routes. Of the four, one lost his nerve and went home. The other three stood waiting, grasping their oddly wrapped packages.

Returning from the review, the imperial party moved swiftly along the snow-covered quay of Catherine Canal. The carriage carrying the tsar and the grand duke was preceded by a screen of six mounted Cossacks. Behind them came three sleighs carrying security officials. Positioned against the iron railing along the canal was nineteen-year-old Nikolai Rysakov —a student, a member of the People's Will, and one of the assigned bomb-throwers.

As the tsar and his retinue approached, Rysakov unwrapped his bomb. When the tsar's carriage was opposite him, he hurled the bomb under the horses' legs. There was a loud explosion, a sheet of flame, a haze of blue smoke. When the smoke cleared, a Cossack and a passing delivery boy lay mortally wounded in the snow. A hundred yards or so down the quay the tsar's coachman finally managed to stop the imperial carriage. Miraculously, it seemed, the tsar stepped from the door, determined to inspect the scene of the explosion. He walked back to the railing, where police were holding Rysakov. Approaching the terrorist, the tsar said, "So you threw the bomb!"

"Yes," replied Rysakov.

"What is your name?" asked the tsar.

"Glasov."

"A fine fellow," said the tsar contemptuously. Turning his back on the terrorist, he said to a police official, "Thanks to God, I am safe."

From the grip of his captors, Rysakov called out, "It may still be too soon to thank God!"

The tsar agreed to return to the palace in one of the sleighs that had been following his carriage. As he walked along the quay, he approached Ignaty Grinevitsky, a twenty-six-year-old engineering student and the second of the bomb-throwers. Grinevitsky hurled his bomb at the tsar's feet. There was another deafening blast, a sheet of flame, fragments of snow, earth, and stone. There were screams, groans, and then silence. When the blue haze lifted, twenty persons lay injured or dying. Among the dying were both the terrorist and his victim.

The tsar was lying on his back, his head propped on the railing, his uniform burned and tattered, his body gushing blood. His legs were shattered, arteries were severed, blood darkened the snow. Among the bystanders who helped the police lift the tsar into a sleigh was Ivan Yemelyanov, a twenty-six-year-old carpenter, and the bomb-thrower who would have acted next, had Grinevitsky failed. The tsar was driven to the palace, where he was given Holy Communion. Then, less than three hours after he had left the palace, he died.

THE OUTCOME

When news of the assassination reached the prison in which Nechaev was held, he said to his guards: "Now you see I was speaking the truth. We have killed him. I was the first to warn you." From then on, he was shown no mercy. Writing implements were taken from him and he was shackled. With his body rotting away, and steel biting into his flesh, he wrote a savage attack on the prison warden with a nail dipped in his own blood. But it was the end of his conspiracies, and he died four years later, in 1885.

For the terrorists who killed the tsar, the end came more quickly. Zhelyabov, Perovskaya, Rysakov, and two others were executed before a crowd of one hundred thousand several months after the assassination. Khalturin, the carpenter, was caught and hanged the following year. The irony of the murder was that on the eve of his assassination—although this was not known at the time—Alexander II had agreed to an important first step on the road to constitutional government. His son and heir, Alexander III, abandoned his father's intention and ruled Russia with unswerving absolutism. In the repression that followed the assassination of Alexander II, the People's Will was virtually, though not entirely, destroyed. Six years later their members, who included Lenin's seventeen-year-old brother, would attempt to assassinate Alexander III. Their effort was unsuccessful and they, too, were hanged.

ANARCHIST TERRORISM
Inspired by Bakunin, Nechaev, and other voices of terrorism, the People's Will believed that the state could be "cleansed," or reformed, through violence. In a letter to Alexander III, written ten days after the death of his father, the People's Will demanded: ". . . the summoning of representatives of all the Russian peoples to consider the existing social and economic order and to remodel it in and with the peoples' desires— freedom of the press, freedom of speech and assembly, free elections."

Unlike the People's Will, the anarchists were unconditionally committed to terrorism as a means of destroying government altogether. Inspired by Bakunin and Nechaev, anarchist terrorists would dominate the headlines for the rest of the nineteenth century and well into the twentieth. Anarchists bombed theaters and cafés in Paris, Lyons, and Barcelona. They bombed the French Chamber of Deputies and the Paris stock exchange. In the years between 1890 and 1908, they murdered the Empress Elizabeth of Austria-Hungary, Presi-

[37]

dent Carnot of France, King Umberto I of Italy, President McKinley of the United States, King Carlos I of Portugal, and a Spanish prime minister. As the French poet Artur Rimbaud described it, this was "the age of assassins."

None of these acts succeeded in bringing down a government or state. But in 1914, one assassination changed the course of history. On June 28 of that year, the Austrian Archduke Franz Ferdinand and his wife were murdered at Sarajevo, in what is now Yugoslavia. The murder of the heir to the throne of Austria-Hungary led to World War I. The assassin was neither a revolutionary nor an anarchist, but a young nationalist obsessed with the idea of independence for Serbia, which was part of the Austro-Hungarian Empire. Nationalism —not revolution or anarchy—would be the prime motive of terrorists in the new age that began with World War I.

CHAPTER THREE

TERRORISM AND NATIONHOOD

*I was born into a situation in which
violence predominated, and it seemed
that the only way of getting rid of
British rule, with all its injustices, was
by means of a liberation movement.*

*Sean MacBride, former
commander-in-chief,
Irish Republican Army;
winner of the 1974
Nobel Peace Prize*

*A new generation grew up that knew
no fear. We fight, therefore we are.*

*Menachem Begin, former
leader of the Irgun;
former prime minister
of Israel*

Anarchist terrorism peaked, then faded, during the first decade of our century. Anarchists themselves finally repudiated terrorism and violence. But the young Serbian nationalist who fired the shot that led to World War I had not repudiated violence. And the many nationalist and separatist movements active during this period turned increasingly to terrorism as a method of achieving independence. From about 1914 until the 1960s, the history of terrorism is dominated by such nationalist-separatist groups as the Irish Republican Army and the Jewish Palestinian Irgun.

Just as Russia provides the first example of revolutionary terrorism, so Ireland offers the first historic case of nationalist-separatist terrorism. Irish nationalist terrorism has its roots in a long tradition of violence that goes back at least to the 1790s, when it was strongly influenced by the French Revolution. Ever since then, each generation in Ireland has seen assassinations, bombings, uprisings or guerrilla campaigns—all aimed at driving the English from Ireland and achieving independence.

In the 1860s a group called the Fenian Brotherhood was responsible for the bombing of Clerkenwell prison in England, killing twelve persons and wounding more than a hundred. In 1882 members of the secret Invincible Society stabbed and killed Lord Frederick Cavendish, chief secretary for Ireland, and his undersecretary, in Phoenix Park in Dublin. The "Dynamiters," who operated in the 1870s and 1880s, developed a fantastic scheme for invading England. Their most daring leader, William Mackey Lomasney, lost his life in an attempt to bomb London Bridge in 1884.

Early in this century, Irish nationalists were organized openly and legally as the Sinn Fein party—"sinn fein" being the Gaelic phrase for "we ourselves." Secretly the nationalists were organized as the Irish Republican Army, or IRA, which stepped up its terrorism against the English after Britain went to war with Germany in 1914. To a growing number of Irish nationalists, violence seemed the only course open to them, and England's involvement in World War I seemed to hold new promise for their cause. Among those who thought so was young Sean MacBride.

The most noted of IRA leaders, Sean MacBride held every rank possible, including commander-in-chief. Not unlike other IRA recruits, he had been born into a strongly nationalistic family. His father, John MacBride, was a major in the IRA. His mother, Maud Gonne, had founded the nationalistic Daughters of Ireland. Twice Sean had helped her to escape from British prisons. So it seemed natural to him, at the age of fourteen, to join the IRA: "It seemed . . . the only way of getting rid of British rule."

EASTER 1916

During Easter Week of 1916, with Germany's assistance, the IRA led an uprising in Dublin and other parts of Ireland. Like earlier insurrections, the Easter Rising of 1916 failed. Its leaders, including Major John MacBride, were tried, convicted, and executed for treason. But the effect of the uprising was an overwhelming resurgence of Irish nationalism, which the poet William Butler Yeats described in "Easter, 1916":

> We know their dream; enough
> To know they dreamed and are dead;
> And what if excess of love
> Bewildered them till they died?
> I write it out in a verse—
> MacDonagh and MacBride
> And Connolly and Pearse
> Now and in time to be,
> Wherever green is worn,
> Are changed, changed utterly:
> A terrible beauty is born.

[42]

The Easter Rising was the catalyst for a series of events that led to an undeclared war with Britain. In 1919 the Sinn Fein members of the British Parliament declared Ireland's independence, organizing a Parliament of their own—the Dail. Their defiance marked the beginning of open conflict, which lasted for three years. Terrorism in this case bordered on guerrilla warfare, and the active support or sympathy of the people gave the IRA an advantage that other terrorist groups usually have lacked.

The IRA made its acts of terrorism appear to be retaliatory action against British oppression in Ireland. Among the means the IRA used were shooting the police, attacking police barracks, ambushing British soldiers, and destroying the property of the English and of Irish sympathizers with English rule.

Michael Collins, chief-of-staff of the IRA, and a popular hero during the struggle, formulated this strategy of selective terrorism:

> We struck at individuals, and by so doing we cut their lines of communication, and we shook their morale. We conducted the conflict, so far as possible, according to the rules of war. Only the armed forces and the spies and criminal agents of the British government were attacked.

Acting on this strategy, IRA squads descended on the "safe houses" of sixteen British undercover agents in Dublin, killing them all and damaging the British intelligence net severely. But even more damaging to the British cause were the reprisals that followed. British soldiers and the Black and Tans—reservists called up for service in Ireland—opened fire on ten thousand spectators at a soccer match in Dublin, killing seventeen.

"THOSE WHO CAN ENDURE"
In another incident, three members of the IRA were arrested by the British and shot "while trying to escape." Ultimately, such acts as these proved unacceptable to the British public, and a consensus developed: if Ireland could be ruled only through counterterrorism, then it was not worth ruling. Frustrated by its inability to win by conventional means,

Britain sought a negotiated settlement. Unable to win, the IRA had refused to lose. Terence MacSwiney, an IRA leader who had died during a hunger strike in 1920, had foreseen the outcome: "It is not those who can inflict the most suffering who will win, but those who can endure the most."

In December 1920, Sinn Fein representatives Arthur Griffith and Michael Collins met with British representatives to negotiate a treaty. Seventeen-year-old Sean MacBride, by now a veteran of the struggle, served as Collins' aide-de-camp during the negotiations. According to the terms of the treaty, the six Protestant counties in the North would remain under direct British rule, while the twenty-six Catholic counties in the South would be given dominion status as the Irish Free State. The Free State would have its own parliament and be completely self-governing, but like other dominions, it would acknowledge the British monarch as its symbolic head.

Now—if the treaty were accepted—there would be two Irelands, one of which remained part of Great Britain. Would the IRA militants accept the treaty? As Lord Birkenhead, the British negotiator, signed the treaty, he remarked to Michael Collins: "I may have signed my political death warrant tonight." And Collins replied, "I may have signed my actual death warrant."

Six months later, Michael Collins lay dead on an Irish roadside, a bullet through his head. His death was the work of fanatics who regarded the treaty as a betrayal. And even though the Irish Dail accepted the treaty by a vote of 64 to 57, the extremists refused to go along with the majority. One of the unreconciled republican leaders, Eamon De Valera, argued that the people, meaning the Dail, "had no right to do wrong."

And so civil war succeeded the war with Britain, with the Irish Free State pitted against the extremist wing of the IRA. Terrorism began anew, with a familiar round of bombings, assassinations, and arson. Fighting continued for nearly a year, until De Valera called for a cease-fire in 1923. In that same year the IRA went underground, and it was outlawed by the Free State in 1931.

PALESTINIAN TERRORISM
In the 1940s, during World War II, a new wave of terrorism took shape, this time in the colonies of Britain, France, and the

other colonial powers. Nationalist groups in these colonies began to agitate more militantly for separation and independence. More often than not, agitation led to terrorism, guerrilla warfare, or both. And the rest of the decade was dominated by the anticolonial terrorism of nationalist-separatist movements in what would now be called "the third world."

The first anticolonial struggle of this period came in Palestine, which was administered by Great Britain under a mandate first from the League of Nations, then from the United Nations. Since the 1890s Zionists, who are Jewish nationalists, had regarded Palestine as a likely Jewish homeland. The earliest Jewish immigrants arrived at the turn-of-the-century, but just as Jewish colonization began, Arab nationalism began its awakening. The Arabs of Palestine began to see the Jews as a threat to their own aspirations for statehood. There were conflicts between Jewish and Arab Palestinians as early as the 1920s.

The year 1933, which marked Hitler's coming to power, proved to be the turning point for the Zionist cause. Jewish emigration from Europe had become a life-or-death matter. In 1933 thirty thousand Jews arrived in Palestine from Europe. The next year, more than forty thousand arrived. And the following year, more than sixty thousand. At this rate of growth, the Jewish population of Palestine would again double within a few years.

The Arabs implored the British to halt Jewish immigration, but the British refused. Once more, Palestine became a battleground between Arab and Jew. Powerless to stop the conflict, the British proposed a partition of Palestine. There would be an Arab area, a Jewish area, and an international zone. The proposal was rejected by the Arabs and given an ambiguous reception by the Jews. The British dropped the scheme.

For their part, the Jews were preoccupied with what was taking place in Europe, which stood on the brink of war. In 1939 Hitler was preparing to invade Poland, the home of three million Jews. Britain was pledged to go to war in support of Poland, and as the British mobilized their army, it seemed as if they were the Jews' only hope.

But at all costs, the British wanted to discourage Arab

[45]

cooperation with Nazi Germany in the strategic Middle East. And so in 1939, on the eve of World War II, the British restricted the number of Jews who could enter Palestine. In practice, British policy was relentless. Jews without official entry permits were turned away—in some cases, returned to Germany.

A CRUEL DILEMMA

The war presented every Jew with an agonizing conflict of loyalties. While tens of thousands of Palestinian Jews were joining the British army to fight Hitler, thousands of illegal immigrants were entering Palestine in defiance of the British. Eager to defeat the Nazis, many Palestinians felt they had to resist British immigration policy as well.

Among Palestinian Jews, there were many differences between moderates and radicals that persist in Israeli politics today. The principal groups recognized by the British were the Jewish Agency, which was in charge of immigration, and its military arm, the Haganah, a militia-style organization that emphasized self-defense. Both cooperated with the British with the understanding that Britain would support the creation of a Jewish state after the war.

But there were militant nationalists who wanted independence immediately so that they could open up the gates to Jewish refugees from Europe. In 1937 a group of extreme militants seceded from the Haganah to form the Irgun Zvai Leumi, or National Military Organization. One of the Irgun's leaders, Menachem Begin, would later become leader of the Likud party and prime minister of Israel. With no more than one-thousand to fifteen hundred members, the Irgun proposed to expel Britain from Palestine.

The Irgun's strategy was to attack British property interests, forcing Britain to move troops from fronts in Africa and Asia to Palestine. For the most part, the Irgun limited its attacks to such targets as army installations. After the war began in September 1939, the Irgun called off operations for a while, believing that a Nazi victory would be a worse evil than British domination. It was then that a more extreme splinter group of the Irgun formed the Fighters for the Freedom of Israel—also known as LEHI or the Stern gang.

Led by Avraham Stern, the Stern gang wanted to continue and intensify the Irgun's campaign of terror against the British. Terrorism, insisted Stern, could educate and inspire the overly cautious Jews of Palestine. For a while, the group explored the possibility of cooperating with the Nazis, but the opportunity never materialized. The group's early acts were mainly gun-fights with British military personnel. In one of these gun-fights, Stern was killed, and for a while his movement seemed near collapse. But his followers built LEHI, which in 1944 attracted world attention with the murder of Lord Moyne, the British minister of state for the Near East.

By killing Lord Moyne in Cairo, Egypt—an Arab state also occupied by the British—LEHI believed it would reveal to both Arabs and Jews alike that they were common victims of British imperialism. Although the act attracted international attention, it failed to attract wide sympathy from Jews or Arabs.

When the war ended in 1945, Jews expected the British immediately to reopen Palestine to unrestricted immigration. When they did not, the Haganah, the Irgun, and LEHI agreed to collaborate—in spite of their differences—in the newly formed Jewish Resistance Movement. Together, terrorists of the three organizations attacked railroads, ports, and ships; they kidnapped British officers and freed illegal Jewish immigrants who had been interned by the British.

TERRORISM AGAINST ISRAEL

Over the next two years, events moved swiftly and favorably for the Jews. It seemed that terrorism had ended. In 1947 the United Nations General Assembly adopted a resolution on Palestine recommending partition into an Arab state, a Jewish state, and the international city of Jerusalem. On May 14, 1948, on the day before the British mandate expired, the Jews proclaimed the state of Israel. On May 15 the armies of Transjordan, Egypt, Syria, Lebanon, and Iraq, assisted by contingents from Saudi Arabia and Yemen, invaded the new state in defiance of the UN resolution. Israel defeated the Arab armies, occupying land that had been allotted to the never-proclaimed Arab state, and increasing its own territory by some 40 percent.

This is how matters stood in the summer of 1948, when a United Nations truce was in effect and UN mediator Count Folke Bernadotte arrived in Jerusalem. LEHI and other extremists feared that Israel's government might make an agreement not to Israel's advantage. And so on September 17 a four-man assassination squad dressed in Israeli army uniforms stopped Bernadotte's car, thrust a submachine gun through the window, and opened fire, killing both Bernadotte and his aide. The Israeli government was stunned. Fearful of world reaction, it rounded up the members of LEHI and imprisoned its leaders. But if Bernadotte was dead, so was the possibility of any UN-sponsored compromise.

One of the Irgun's last acts was the massacre of 250 Arabs at the village of Deir Yassin. Again, Menachem Begin attributed the loss of life to the victims' failure to heed a warning to evacuate. By now Irgun terrorism had thoroughly alienated the rest of the Jewish community. On June 2, 1948, an agreement between the Irgun and the Israeli government went into effect, providing for the integration of the Irgun's fifteen thousand members into the Haganah. Yet on June 23, Begin went ahead with plans to unload arms intended for the Irgun from a ship in Tel Aviv harbor. What followed was a pitched battle between Israeli army units and the Irgun. Government forces sank the ship and killed fifteen terrorists, effectively crushing the movement.

But the Irgun's influence was by no means ended. Its strategy and innovative methods have been studied and imitated by terrorists in Vietnam, Uruguay, French Canada, Ulster, and elsewhere. And Arabs, too, would heed the lessons and the experience of the Jewish terrorists.

PART II

TERRORISM SINCE THE 1960s

CHAPTER
FOUR

MENTORS

What modern capitalists produce, above all, are their own gravediggers. The fall of the capitalists and the victory of the workers are equally inevitable.

Karl Marx and Friedrich Engels, Communist Manifesto, *1848*

Today the East Wind prevails over the West Wind. That is, the forces of socialism have become overwhelmingly superior to the forces of imperialism.

Mao Zedong, in a speech to a meeting of Communist parties, Moscow, 1957

Throughout the 1950s and into the 1960s, the guerrilla up-staged the terrorist. Mao Zedong, Ho Chi Minh, Fidel Castro, and other guerrilla leaders showed how a revolt could begin in some distant province, gradually gain strength, and finally en-velop the major cities. This has been the pattern in China, Algeria, Cuba, and Vietnam—where guerrillas had not only defeated the French, but would defeat the Americans as well. In Latin America Ché Guevara made "One More Vietnam!" his rallying cry, hoping to launch a guerrilla war to entrap American "imperialists." But guerrilla warfare failed miserably in Peru and Colombia. And in 1967 Guevara himself was killed in an abortive attempt to organize guerrillas in Bolivia.

In the meantime, the United States had become increas-ingly involved in Vietnam. Many millions of people throughout the world, including Americans, sided with the Vietnamese in this conflict, and a worldwide antiwar movement developed. The movement succeeded in radicalizing many persons, mov-ing them from support for the United States to opposition; from moderation to activism; and in some cases, from activism to violence. Nowhere was this process more evident than on American college campuses.

James Kunen describes the process of student radicalization in *The Strawberry Statement*. In April 1968 students at Columbia University in New York City seized several uni-versity buildings to protest the role of the university and the academic community in the war. After about a week, the police were called in, and Kunen was among those arrested:

. . . [T]he bust finally came. Information filtered in via walkie talkie and runner—descriptions of people being

[53]

dragged by their hair down stairs, clubbings, blood being spilled. The cops took one building after another by force. . . .

They were swearing and grunting, working at cutting the hoses and ropes around the door, pulling the furniture down piece by piece. I thought when they got to me, they'd kill me. People up and down the stairwell were beating a rhythm on overturned wastepaper baskets. The whole thing had everyone's blood racing. . . .

The police grabbed me and broke through our linked arms. Then, holding on to my feet and arms, they threw me under a tree. The paddy wagons were at the Sundial, the whole place was floodlit and illuminated. Even at a night baseball game, when the night is suddenly turned to day, an exhilarating feeling overcomes me: "This is history." An enormous crowd, densely packed, shouted: "Strike! Strike! Strike!" with their hands in V's waving back and forth in the air.

The scene was repeated across the United States and around the world. Soon after the Columbia riots, students in Paris began an even more violent protest that nearly toppled the government of President Charles de Gaulle. In these and similar actions, students and others who had begun their opposition to the war with nonviolent protests crossed the boundary into violence.

The failure of guerrilla warfare and the growing radicalization of opinion and behavior caused by the war in Vietnam were two reasons for the resurgence of terrorism in the mid-1960s. Most, but not all, of these new terrorists were anarchists or revolutionaries seeking to overturn the established order. But regardless of their political objectives, all were influenced to some extent by the same theorists and strategists.

MARX AND THE MARXISTS

On occasion both Karl Marx and his collaborator, Friedrich Engels, had condoned acts of terrorism as positive expressions of revolutionary fervor. But in principle, Marx and Engels condemned the "foolishness which is to be found in every conspiracy." They denounced the "purposeless propaganda of the deed" of the anarchists. Of the Russian anarchist Bakunin, Engels wrote that only a police agent could have identified revolution with individual and collective murder. For Marx and Engels, revolutions were made by classes, not by conspirators. Terrorists they described variously as "cannibals," "cowards," and "stupid fanatics."

Marx's Russian followers, Vladimir Lenin and Leon Trotsky, believed that revolution required patient organization of the workers by the Communist party. "Without the working people," wrote Lenin, "all bombs are powerless, utterly powerless." Both Lenin and Trotsky argued that terrorism made organizational and political work among the people more difficult; that "easy tactics" never proved worthwhile and might even create the impression that revolution was a simple matter. Significantly, however, Trotsky once said that terrorism might have a future in the colonial world, where it could play a role in the "political awakening" of the masses.

Despite their generally negative view of terrorism, Marxist theorists were a major influence on terrorists of the 1960s and 1970s. While ignoring passages in the Marxist scriptures that condemned terrorism, Irish Republicans and Black Panthers alike could cite passages that condoned it. More importantly, terrorists discovered in Marxism a basic world view: the conviction, for example, that "one fact is common to all ages— the exploitation of one part of society by another." They believed, as Lenin had, that capitalism had reached its final stage—imperialism—and was now ripe for revolution. And they claimed to see, as Trotsky had foreseen, the decisive conflict with capitalism taking shape in the third world.

For their analysis of the contemporary world situation, the terrorists looked to other Marxists for inspiration. They were particularly impressed by Mao Zedong's insistence that the United States, the leader of world capitalism, was a "paper tiger" that could be provoked, involved in conflict, and destroyed. Mao regarded guerrilla warfare as the means of destroying the capitalist system, and he, too, expressed strong reservations about the use of terrorism. Terrorists ignored these reservations and emphasized other Maoist thoughts.

In 1966, *Quotations from Chairman Mao*—or the "little

red book," as it was popularly called—was printed in many languages in Peking and distributed worldwide, becoming a familiar fixture in terrorist cells. Such Maoist maxims as these shaped the outlook of a generation of terrorists across the globe:

> Classes struggle, some classes triumph, others are eliminated. Such is history, such is the history of civilization for thousands of years.

> Revolutions and revolutionary wars are inevitable in class society, and without them it is impossible to accomplish any leap in social development or to overthrow the reactionary ruling classes.

> A revolution is not a dinner party, or writing an essay, or painting a picture, or doing embroidery. It cannot be so refined, so leisurely and gentle, so temperate, kind, courteous, restrained and magnanimous. A revolution is an insurrection: an act of violence by which one class overthrows another.

> Every communist must grasp the truth: Political power grows out of the barrel of a gun.

ENTER THE "URBAN GUERRILLA"

Marx and Lenin shaped the world view of the new terrorists. Mao shaped their analysis of the contemporary scene. Abraham Guillén and Carlos Marighella provided them with the strategy and tactics of the "urban guerrilla," a term they used in place of "terrorist."

Abraham Guillén, who was born in Spain in 1913, fought to defend the Spanish Republic against fascists led by Francisco Franco. When the fascists came to power in 1939, Guillén was sentenced to death. His sentence was commuted to twenty years' imprisonment, of which he served nearly ten. He escaped in 1945 to France, where he lived for three years before moving to Argentina and finally to Uruguay. He was not a terrorist, but he was sympathetic to the cause of terrorism, and he knew personally many Latin American terrorists.

In 1966 Guillén published *Strategy of the Urban Guerrilla*, which proved to be an immediate and strong influence on terrorism. In *Strategy* and other writings, Guillén pointed out that Latin America has the fastest rate of urbanization in the world; therefore, a strategy that had worked in China and Cuba could not be successful in, say, Venezuela or Brazil. He wrote:

> If seventy percent of a country's population is urban, the demography and the economy must dictate the specific rules of the strategy of revolutionary combat. The center of operations should never be in the mountains or in the villages, but in the largest cities, where the population is large enough to form the army of the revolution. . . . What is important is not to win space, but rather to destroy the enemy and to endure longer.

To destroy the enemy, Guillén advocated a strategy of progressive harassment: "The strategy of the artichoke is the most prudent one for urban or rural guerrillas: to eat the enemy bit by bit, and through brief and surprise encounters of encirclement and annihilation, to live off the enemy's arms, munitions and paramilitary effects."

Like Guillén, Carlos Marighella played a major role in shaping the strategy and methods of modern terrorism. Marighella was a Brazilian communist who broke with his party to become a terrorist. In 1969 Marighella published *The Minimanual of the Urban Guerrilla*, which has been treasured in its many translations by terrorists around the world. Like Guillén, Marighella defines the principal task of the terrorist as harassment: ". . . to distract, to wear out, to demoralize the militarists, the military dictatorship and its repressive forces, and also to attack and destroy the wealth and property of the North Americans, the foreign managers, and the Brazilian upper class."

Although Marighella lists a number of acts that the terrorist might accomplish, two types of act are essential in his strategy of "wearing down" the authorities—killing chiefs of police and military officers, and expropriating government and capitalist resources, especially arms and money. Such acts, said Marighella, would create a political crisis. The terrorist can then turn the political crisis into armed conflict through acts "that will alienate the masses." Once alienated, the masses "will revolt against the army and the police and blame them for this state of things. . . ."

Marighella emphasized the propaganda effect of terrorism, describing how terrorists might manipulate the media to demoralize and undermine the government:

Airplanes diverted in flight by revolutionary action, moving ships and trains assaulted and seized—all can be used solely for their propaganda effect.

The war of nerves, or psychological warfare, is an aggressive technique based on the direct or indirect use of mass means of communication and news transmitted orally in order to demoralize the government.

In psychological warfare, the government is always at a disadvantage since it imposes censorship on the media and winds up in a defensive position by not allowing anything against it to filter through.

More than any others, it was Guillén and Marighella who updated and refined the strategy and tactics of terrorism, adapting them to the conditions of the mid-1960s. Their teachings would be put into practice first in Latin America, then in North America, Europe, and elsewhere.

JUSTIFYING TERRORISM

Terrorists since the 1960s have shared other influences besides the Marxists, the guerrilla theorists, and the new theorists of urban terrorism. Among these other influences are Bakunin and Nechaev; the French philosopher Jean-Paul Sartre; the Algerian psychiatrist Frantz Fanon; and the Iranian Moslem religious leader Ayatollah (which means "holy one") Ruhollah Khomeini.

Bakunin and Nechaev offer the would-be terrorist a glorification of violence, as well as what some persons take to be its moral justification. Both Sartre and Fanon attempted to update the moral justification. Sartre—in his philosophy, fiction, and drama—described revolutionary violence as the means through

[58]

which individuals might liberate themselves from oppression and passivity. Fanon, who served as chief propagandist for the Algerian National Liberation Front, applied Sartre's notion of "liberating violence" to nationality groups oppressed by colonialism. Fanon argued that violence is essential for the colonized to purge themselves of the degrading effects of colonialism. He wrote: "Violence is a cleansing force, freeing the colonized from their inferiority complex and from despair and inaction. It makes them fearless and restores their self-respect."

The Ayatollah Ruhollah Khomeini found a justification for terrorism in the Koran, the holy book of Moslems. As an exile in France in the 1960s and 1970s, Khomeini advocated terrorism as a means of replacing the monarchy with an Islamic republic. After the shah was overthrown in 1979, Khomeini returned to Iran, established an Islamic "republic," and used terrorism against both internal and external opponents. Khomeini's accomplishment has since served as an inspiration to fanatics who seek to establish Islamic "republics" elsewhere.

From these theorists and practitioners of terrorism has come a loosely knit body of beliefs from which terrorists since the 1960s have borrowed freely, according to their particular orientation and needs. From these and others have come the ideas that have mobilized two generations of terrorists—from Canada to Argentina, from Japan to the United States to the Middle East.

CHAPTER
FIVE

VICIOUS CYCLES

TERRORISM IN
LATIN AMERICA

*If I were younger, I would be with
you in Argentina, throwing bombs
and advancing the cause of justice
with my own hands.*

*Juan Perón, former and future
president of Argentina, in
a message from exile to his
supporters in Argentina, 1970*

*It is an eye for an eye,
and a tooth for a tooth.*

Carlos Marighella,
The Minimanual of the
Urban Guerrilla, *1969*

*The way of armed struggle is adopted
when one is fully convinced that it is
the way to overthrow those who hold
on to power—that power that gives
them all their profits, privileges,
and pleasures at the cost of the
efforts of others.*

*"Urbano," a leader of
Uruguay's Tupamaros,
in an interview in*
Cuba Socialista, *1970*

Carlos Marighella, the son of an Italian immigrant and a black Brazilian woman, was known as "the ebony giant." He joined the Brazilian Communist party in 1928, at the age of sixteen, going on to become a member of its executive committee. In 1945 he served briefly as a member of the Brazilian House of Representatives until the Communist party was outlawed. In 1964 he was arrested while addressing a rally at a movie theater in Rio. In the riot that followed, the police shot him three times in the stomach. He recovered and escaped from the infirmary where he was being held.

He became increasingly disillusioned with the Communist party for its nonviolent tactics. He resigned from its executive committee in 1966 to protest its "lack of militancy." The following year he went to Cuba to attend the Conference of Latin American Solidarity, and from Havana he called for armed struggle against Brazil's military regime, which had seized power in 1964. He returned secretly to Brazil in 1967. In 1969 he was expelled by the Communist party and denounced for his advocacy of violence. But by then the party meant very little to Marighella, who had decided on an independent course of action. In that same year, 1969, Marighella launched a campaign of terrorism in the streets of Rio and São Paulo.

THE BEGINNING
AND THE END
From 1968 to 1971 two major terrorist groups were active in Brazil: the National Liberation Army, or ALN, which was Marighella's group; and the People's Revolutionary Vanguard,

or VPR. In 1968, in one of the first acts of Brazilian terrorists, members of the VPR murdered a U.S. Army captain on a street in São Paulo. A statement by the VPR claimed the act as revenge for Ché Guevara's death. Near the captain's body were found leaflets responding to Guevara's rallying cry: "Brazil is the Vietnam of America."

Another early act of Brazilian terrorists was the expropriation of capital. More than a hundred banks in Brazil's largest cities were robbed by the ALN, the VPR, and other terrorist groups in 1968 and 1969. At the same time, American-owned companies and warehouses were bombed, barracks were burned, and jailbreaks were carried out. In August 1969 Marighella and several other terrorists seized a radio station and broadcast a virulent attack on the military dictatorship.

But it was not until September 1969 that Brazilian terrorism captured the world's attention. On that day, members of Marighella's group collaborated with another group in kidnapping the United States ambassador to Brazil, Charles Elbrick. In return for his release, the terrorists demanded the release of fifteen political prisoners. The military government agreed to the exchange, and the freed prisoners were flown to Mexico. Humiliated, Brazil's junta decided on brutal repression.

Brazil's security forces—the regular police, the political police, and army and navy intelligence units—had in fact developed a response to terrorism that proved effective, as well as instructive. The method emphasized assassination; police "death squads" were authorized to kill known or suspected criminals. Torture had already been institutionalized, and now it could be further justified. After all, said one police chief, "we have to get our information quick or the whole cell will be gone. . . ."

The information police most wanted in 1969 was the whereabouts of Carlos Marighella. In October 1969, the police arrested two men who revealed under torture enough information to plan an operation to capture or kill Marighella. On November 4, in São Paulo, eighty police ambushed and killed Marighella in a shoot-out.

Others carried on the campaign of terror. In 1970 the ALN and the VPR cooperated in the kidnapping of West

Germany's ambassador to Brazil, who was released in exchange for forty political prisoners. Later the same year, the VPR captured Switzerland's ambassador, obtaining the release of seventy more political prisoners. But security forces were closing in, and torture discouraged new recruits. Marighella's successor as leader of the ALN was killed in 1970; and the leader of the VPR, in 1971.

All that Brazil's terrorists accomplished was the hardening of an already repressive dictatorship. Only in 1985 did the armed forces step aside for a civilian president, returning to their historical role of behind-the-scenes control. By insisting that the new civilian president be chosen indirectly by an electoral college, they ensured a government acceptable to themselves. A 1979 amnesty that benefited former terrorists also benefited those who were accused of human rights abuses. Trials of army officers were thus averted. Today, as in the past, the political role of the military seems to be accepted as a fact of Brazilian life.

The lasting influence of Brazilian terrorism is represented by Marighella's *Minimanual of the Urban Guerrilla*. Translated into many languages and banned by some governments, Marighella's teachings have been applied by disciples in Ulster, in the Middle East, and elsewhere. In Brazil they are a distant memory.

THE TUPAMAROS

The National Liberation Movement, or MLN, was active in Uruguay at about the same time that Marighella saw action in Brazil. MLN terrorists, who were known as Tupamaros, were Marxist-Leninists fighting to overthrow Uruguay's government, which then was one of the few democratic governments in Latin America. Deliberately vague as to their political beliefs and objectives, they stressed the need for violence: "Words divide us, actions unite us. There are undoubtedly solutions for the problems of the country, but they will not be achieved without armed struggle."

Most of the Tupamaros were university students who had studied historical cases of terrorism—the French resistance to the Nazis, the FLN's battle for Algiers, and the Irgun's campaign against the British, which they found most relevant to their own situation. One of their leaders, Urbano, recalls: "On the basis of these facts, it was considered practical to launch an experiment in Latin America—a guerrilla force whose action would be centered in the cities, rather than in the countryside."

In the early 1960s the Tupamaros surfaced infrequently, mainly in raids on banks, businesses, and arms stores. They became internationally known through such exploits as giving stolen food and money to the poor. Their membership grew from fifty to five thousand. With growing self-assurance and support, they engaged in major military operations in the late 1960s and early 1970s, seizing public buildings, radio stations, police stations, and airports.

Following the teachings of Carlos Marighella, the Tupamaros at first emphasized the psychological objective of embarrassing and discrediting the government. This it accomplished through its superior operational skills, and through such novel techniques as broadcasting stolen documents that revealed corruption in high places. The strategic objective of Tupamaro terrorism—influenced by Abraham Guillén, as well as by Marighella—was to escalate individual terrorism to mass action that would overthrow the government.

TERRORISM ESCALATES
In 1970, in line with their theory of escalation, the Tupamaros' operations became more violent. They assassinated a number of prominent Uruguayans and attracted world attention with a series of kidnappings. Their most important victim was Sir Geoffrey Jackson, the British ambassador, who was held in a "people's prison" in Montevideo for eight months—much to the embarrassment of the government and the police. Among their other kidnap victims were a Brazilian consul, a U.S. agronomist, and a U.S. police adviser, Daniel Mitrione. When the Uruguayan government refused to bargain for Mitrione's release, the terrorists executed him, explaining: "The logic of the technique of kidnapping to get the release of prisoners has to be followed all the way if it is to remain effective."

By mid-1971, the Tupamaros were at their zenith. Then, as the November elections approached, they toned down their terrorism so as not to harm the prospects of the leftist party.

But when the leftists were soundly defeated, the Tupamaros escalated their violence once more, this time with hit-and-run attacks on army personnel. Unable to curb the violence, the new government called in the army to crush the terrorists. The army succeeded in smashing the Tupamaros. In doing so, the army also destroyed Uruguay's democracy, replacing it in 1973 with a ruthless military regime.

Not until 1985 did another elected president take office in Uruguay, ending twelve years of military rule. One of the greatest challenges confronting Uruguay's new president is to avert a confrontation between the still-powerful armed forces and opposition groups who are pressing for trials of officers accused of human rights violations. The chain of events set in action by the Tupamaros still clouds the prospects for democracy in Uruguay today.

TERRORISM IN ARGENTINA
In 1955 the popular but corrupt demagogue Juan Domingo Perón was ousted from the presidency of Argentina and forced into exile. His nine-year rule was followed by a series of incompetent and repressive civilian and military governments that mismanaged the economy, suppressed political opposition, and finally alienated every sector of society. Although Perónist political parties were outlawed, Perónism remained strong. In the late 1960s, Perón's followers—the Peronistas—joined with other political parties in calling for elections and an end to military rule.

At about the same time, leftist Peronistas began organizing terrorist units known as the Montoneros. And Péron's rightist supporters formed another terrorist group, the Argentine Anti-Communist Alliance, or Triple A. The Montoneros and the Triple A were merely two among hundreds of terrorist groups active in the early 1970s. Coexisting with these two forces were rural and urban Trotskyite terrorists; right-wing Perónist death squads; terrorist groups of the large labor unions; paramilitary army groups dedicated to avenging the murder of their men by other terrorists; parapolice groups of both the left and the right, vying for control of federal and provincial police forces; and terrorist groups of Catholic rightists.

[67]

In 1970 the Montoneros kidnapped and murdered former Argentine president Aramburu. Other terrorists kidnapped a British consul and assassinated a police chief. Isolated and infrequent events rapidly escalated into a frenzy of violence— attacks on police and army installations, airplane hijackings, and the seizure of airfields and radio stations. Each act was justified by its perpetrators in the language of fascist or communist ideology. In reality, terrorism had assumed a life and momentum of its own: terrorism for the sake of terrorism. In an article in the *New Yorker* magazine, Jacobo Timerman, the publisher and editor of the liberal Buenos Aires newspaper *La Opinión*, described the dynamics of Argentine terrorism in the early 1970s:

> The Montoneros assassinated those who were trying to suppress them; those who they believed were trying to suppress them; those whom they regarded as doing nothing to oppose those who suppressed them; those who spoke up against violence of both the Right and the Left. . . . The Triple A engaged in killing Montoneros, or those they assumed to be Montoneros. They murdered liberal politicians, because their demands for legal trials of arrested Montoneros were regarded as a form of complicity. . . . They murdered defense lawyers of arrested Montoneros. . . . And they murdered writers and leftist journalists.

By 1972 the military dictatorship was in crisis, unable to deal with the chaos created by violence. The nation longed for Juan Perón, believing that he—and only he—possessed the authority to restore order. In 1972 the armed forces allowed Perón, then seventy-seven, to return to Argentina. In September 1973 he was elected president, and his wife Isabel, vice-president.

But Perón could not quell the violence. In 1973–74, the Trotskyite People's Revolutionary Army, or ERP, engaged in an unparalleled wave of kidnappings, demanding ransoms for kidnapped executives of Eastman Kodak, Ford, Firestone, Otis Elevator, ITT-Sheraton, and Exxon. (From Exxon alone the ERP reportedly received $14.2 million.) The ERP and other leftist groups who had expected Perón to create a socialist regime denounced him as a traitor. He, in turn, denounced them as an expression of "pathological barbarism." Masses of Perón's former supporters were arrested as traitors, interrogated under torture, and mutilated.

In June 1974, nine months after his election, Perón died of a heart attack. Isabel Perón succeeded her husband as president and remained in power until March 1976, when a military junta took power. Jacobo Timerman was among the supporters of the military coup, believing that the junta could end the violence of left and right. "When the army installed General Jorge Videla in the presidency," wrote Timerman, "the entire nation breathed a sigh of relief."

REIGN OF TERROR REVISITED
Within a year, the military antiterrorist campaign was successful in eliminating the two main terrorist groups. But to achieve order, the regime ignored the law. Arbitrary arrest, denial of habeas corpus, brutal prison conditions, kidnapping, torture, murder, and dismemberment all became accepted techniques. Thousands of men, women, and children disappeared without a trace. Thousands of other suspects were arrested without warrant or charges, and many languished in prisons for five years and more.

The junta's counterterrorism took on a life of its own as military leaders organized their personal domains, each becoming a war lord in the zone under his control. Each officer in charge of a military region had his own prisoners, his own prisons, and his own form of justice. Jacobo Timerman was arrested, interrogated, and tortured by the First Army Corps. As a result of international pressure, he was released and placed under house arrest. Finally, in 1979, he was stripped of his Argentine citizenship and forced into exile.

In exile, Timerman described the unparalleled horror of Argentina's reign of terror:

Entire families disappeared. The bodies were covered with cement and thrown to the bottom of the river. The Plata River, the Paraná River. Sometimes the cement was badly applied, and corpses would wash up along the Argentine and Uruguayan coasts. A mother recog-

[69]

nized her fifteen-year-old son, an Argentine, who appeared on the Uruguayan coast. But that was an accident—the corpses usually vanished forever. The corpses were thrown into old cemeteries, under existing graves, never to be found. The corpses were heaved into the middle of the sea from helicopters. The corpses were dismembered and burned.

When there was mercy, small children were turned over to grandparents. Or presented to childless families. Or sold to childless families. Or taken to Chile, Paraguay, Brazil, and given to childless families.

The situation in Argentina, Timerman wrote, was "more terrible than anything known by our generation in Latin America. It is a struggle between civilization and barbarism."

A DRAMATIC DENOUEMENT

By 1982, after six years of military rule, Argentina's economic condition was deteriorating rapidly. As inflation reached new highs, people became openly critical of the junta's incompetence. And finally, some became critical of the regime's abuses of human rights. Mothers of those who had "disappeared" were openly protesting the disappearance of their children.

In April 1982, in a desperate attempt to revive a failing government, the junta ordered the invasion of the Falkland Islands, a British colony off Argentina's southeast coast. Two months later, a British task force recaptured the islands after more than a thousand men had died in military engagements.

Disgraced by their defeat in battle—the business they knew best—the junta stepped aside in 1983. Under the leadership of President Raul Alfonsin, Argentina returned to civilian rule. In 1985 the nine military officers who had governed Argentina during six violent years stood together in a civilian courtroom accused as criminals. They were charged with murder, torture, and kidnapping in the disappearances of more than nine thousand Argentinians. Although four of the nine were acquitted of the charges, five were found guilty and sentenced to prison terms ranging from seventeen years to life imprisonment. Never before in the history of Latin America had a civilian government held past military rulers responsible for their acts.

In Argentina, Brazil, and Uruguay, terrorism led to the overthrow of semidemocratic governments and the strengthening of repressive military regimes. In each country, ironically, citizens tolerated violence in the name of antiterrorism. Realizing this fact, the Latin juntas refined the techniques of state terrorism that had been introduced during the "reign of terror." They stand in the tradition of Robespierre.

CHAPTER
SIX

STORMING
"THE EMPIRE"

TERRORISM
IN THE
UNITED STATES

*I remember on January 2, 1961—
I was seventeen years old—standing
in downtown Havana, surrounded by a
million people, a million Cubans who
had come to Havana to celebrate the
Cuban revolution. At the end of the six
or seven hours of people celebrating
came a long military parade with guns
and weapons and tanks. I had been
cheering along with everybody else when
I suddenly realized that I was cheering
for tanks and guns, which was
completely opposite to what I had been
brought up to do.*

*My Cuban friend who was standing next
to me saw my eyes fill up with tears.
He looked at me and said, "I understand
what you're feeling. We don't like to have
guns and weapons either, but it's your
country that makes us have to do this."
Three months later the Bay of Pigs
invasion occurred, and I understood
what he meant.*

*Kathy Boudin, a member
of Weather Underground*

Kathy Boudin's passage from student activism to terrorism is the story of the birth, life, and death of the Weather Underground. For Boudin the path began in New York City in the late 1950s, when she was a high school student. Her high school principal recalls her as "rather quiet, thoughtful, sensible and intelligent." A friend remembers her reputation as a good athlete—"a basketball player with a deadly accurate corner jump shot." Even then, as the civil rights movement began, she was an activist, expressing her strong convictions openly and nonviolently. With classmates, she picketed the neighborhood Woolworth's to protest that company's discriminatory hiring policies.

She went to Bryn Mawr College, where she majored in Russian language and literature. But politics and the peace movement consumed an ever growing share of her time and energy. She belonged to SDS—Students for a Democratic Society—which had grown out of the civil rights movement and would soon become an important element in the movement against the war in Vietnam. In 1963, during her junior year in college, Boudin was arrested in Chester, Pennsylvania, for her part in a civil rights demonstration. Her behavior was criticized by some faculty members and students as "disgraceful" to the college. She replied to her critics in a letter published in the Bryn Mawr student newspaper on November 22, 1963, the day of John F. Kennedy's assassination:

It is alleged that being arrested . . . brings discredit on the college. This implies that being arrested is in itself discreditable, and is based on the assumption that law is an end in itself. . . . I believe that law is a means to an end. . . . If desired ends cannot be achieved within the law . . . then new methods must be adopted.

The college newspaper supported Boudin's position, editorializing, "When the issues have been weighed, the demand for human liberty assumes the greatest importance, and civil disobedience is a reasonable and even necessary action."

Boudin took her senior year in Moscow and Leningrad, where she was angered by the apathy of Russian students. "All over the world," she wrote, "students are gathering in revolt, but Soviet students are conspicuous by their absence." In the summer of 1965, after graduation from college, she went to Cleveland as part of an SDS program to organize women on welfare so that they could "assert their rights." The conditions she encountered, and the failure of the program after three years, led Boudin toward a rejection of civil disobedience as a meaningful method of political change. As in Russia a century earlier, a "movement to the people" led to disillusionment.

TURNING POINTS

At the 1968 Democratic convention in Chicago, Vice-President Hubert Humphrey defeated "peace candidate" Eugene McCarthy for the presidential nomination. Like many other groups that formed the mass antiwar movement, SDS regarded the nomination of Humphrey as a betrayal. There were massive sit-ins, demonstrations, and counterdemonstrations in Chicago during the week of the convention. And there was violence. At the Palmer House Hotel, where many of the Democratic delegates were staying, Kathy Boudin was arrested for loosing a stink bomb.

By now she had apparently become convinced that change was impossible without violence. In 1969, she and Eleanor Raskin wrote *The Bust Book*, "a handbook for all political prisoners." In the introduction they wrote, "The cop and judge wear different uniforms, but they serve the same system we seek to destroy." The year 1969 marked the decisive step—for Kathy Boudin and for SDS. And for both, the issue was terrorism.

With Richard Nixon's inauguration as president in January 1969, the antiwar movement saw no prospects for peace in Vietnam. Yet the movement had lost its momentum and splintered over the question of what to do next. SDS met to consider this question in Chicago in June 1969—in what proved to be the last and most momentous of its annual conventions. By then the group had already fragmented into many factions, including Marxists, Leninists, Maoists, anarchists, and others. After bitter disputes on strategy, the organization formally split.

The most important group to emerge from the split was the Weathermen, which took its name from a line in Bob Dylan's "Subterranean Homesick Blues": "You don't need a weatherman to know which way the wind blows." (Later the group changed its name to the Weather Underground because of the sexism implied by the original name.) Before adjourning, the new group scheduled its first annual "national action" for the second week of October 1969, in Chicago. That was the week the trial of the "Chicago eight" would begin, its defendants charged with the acts of violence that had occurred at the 1968 Democratic convention. With national attention focused on Chicago, the group hoped to gain publicity and popular support.

"DAYS OF RAGE"
That first national action of the Weather Underground would become known as "the days of rage." In a four-day rampage, some four hundred members of the group, using clubs and chains, broke shop windows and smashed parked cars in Chicago's business district. They engaged more than a thousand police in a dozen or more battles at intersections. A charge by one-hundred women in crash helmets—Boudin among them—seriously damaged an army induction center. When the action was ended, six members had been hit with buckshot, and sixty-eight had been arrested. There had been nationwide publicity, but the hoped-for popular support did not develop.

Members of the Weather Underground came together for a final public meeting in December 1969, in the black ghetto in Flint, Michigan. There they held a "national war council," surrounded by pictures of Ho Chi Minh, Ché Guevara, Fidel Castro, and Malcolm X. They debated and adopted a strategy of terrorism, having all but abandoned their hope of organizing a mass, popular movement. One of those present at the Flint meeting was Mark Rudd, who had been one of the leaders of the 1968 student uprising at Columbia University.

Rudd argued that violence had both educational and publicity value: "The struggle activity—the actions of our movement—demonstrates our existence and strength to people in a material way. Seeing it happen, people give it more weight in their thinking." And another member, Bernadine Dohrn, who had engineered the split from SDS, rejected nonviolence as an "excuse for not struggling. To not act, to not do anything," she said, "or to not do as much as you can do—whatever it is—is violent, is criminal, is complicity."

The next news of the Weather Underground came three months later, in March 1970. In New York City, five members of the organization were using a town house owned by the father of a member as a bomb factory. There were at least sixty sticks of dynamite in the basement workshop. Someone apparently misconnected a wire while making an "antipersonnel" bomb, and a violent explosion demolished the building. Three terrorists were killed instantly and two escaped—Kathy Boudin and Cathy Wilkerson.

Boudin and Wilkerson were upstairs when the blast occurred. Dazed and shaken, they fought their way out of the ruins through a collapsed floor. They were taken in by a neighbor, who gave them clothing, and as fire engines and police cars converged on the scene, they escaped. Boudin later said, "One of the amazing things in the days following was riding the subways or watching TV and seeing our pictures all around, knowing we were being looked for, and knowing that they weren't able to find us."

"A DECLARATION OF WAR"
In May 1970, the Weather Underground issued a statement that it called "a declaration of war":

Within the next 14 days we will attack a symbol or institution of American injustice. This is the way we

[78]

celebrate the example of Eldridge Cleaver and H. Rap Brown and all black revolutionaries who first inspired us by their fight behind enemy lines for the liberation of their people. Never again will they fight alone.

Nineteen days later, the group planted a bomb at the headquarters of the New York City Police Department, inflicting moderate damage. The next year, they planted a bomb under the barbershop in the U.S. Capitol building, explaining that they wanted "to call attention to the fact that . . . nobody in Congress was taking an honest or a principled or a human position, and doing anything about ending the war in Vietnam." Between 1970 and 1975, the Weather Underground was responsible for at least twenty bombings.

In 1974 the group announced plans to expand its operations to include both clandestine operations and participation in an above-ground support group, which it called the Prairie Fire Organizing Committee: "Here is Prairie Fire, our political ideology, a strategy for anti-imperialism and revoluton inside the imperial U.S. . . . A single spark can start a prairie fire."

The "Prairie Fire" statement defined the Weather Underground's strategy of terrorism, which reflected the influence of Guillén and Marighella.

We are a guerrilla organization. We are communist women and men, underground in the U.S. for more than four years. Our enemy is U.S. imperialism, the enemy of all humankind. Our goal is to attack imperialism's ability to exploit and wage war against all oppressed peoples. . . . We must weaken and at least partly destroy the empire. . . . We are strategically situated in the nerve centers of the international empire, where the institutions and symbols of imperial power are concentrated. The cities will be a major battleground.

But there were no major battles—only infrequent and ineffective bombings. In 1975 five Weatherpeople—Kathy Boudin, Cathy Wilkerson, Bernadine Dohrn, Billy Ayers, and Jeff Jones—appeared in a film called *Underground,* an effort to explain their politics to a large audience. By then, living in a world of false identities and illusions, they were unnoticed and unheeded. At about that time, leaders of the group began to talk about alternatives to violence, including giving up.

In 1977 Mark Rudd became the first of the movement's leaders to surrender. He was fined $2,000 and given two years' probation. Cathy Wilkerson surrendered in 1980, pleaded guilty to possession of dynamite, and began serving a three-year sentence in prison. In December 1980 Bernardine Dohrn surrendered, was fined $1,500 and placed on probation for three years.

A diehard faction, including Kathy Boudin, stayed in hiding, still apparently committed to armed violence. Little is known of the group's activities during this period and not until 1981 would they again receive national attention.

At 3:55 P.M. on October 20, 1981, a red van pulled up behind a Brink's armored car at the Nanuet National Bank in Nanuet, New York. Opening fire with automatic weapons, the robbers killed one guard, wounded two others, and made off with $1,585,000. Minutes later, one of the group's getaway vehicles was halted at a roadblock. There was another shootout in which two police officers were killed and another wounded. An off-duty policeman drove into what he described as "a firefight, like I was back in Vietnam." He saw a woman running down the highway, gave chase, and caught her. He yelled to the woman, "Who are you? Who are you with?" She answered, "I didn't shoot him; he did." She was unarmed, but did not surrender without a struggle. She was Kathy Boudin.

As investigators traced vehicles abandoned by the bank robbers to "safe houses," they discovered evidence that more than one holdup was planned, and that others perhaps had been carried out. They also discovered evidence suggesting that the Weather Underground had formed a "military alliance" with another terrorist group, the Black Liberation Army, and that the bank robbery may have been a joint operation. Police recovered weapons, ammunition, walkie-talkies, floor plans for several Manhattan police stations, and a "hit list" of police officers.

Three days after the Nanuet robbery, police spotted a car with a license plate linked to one of the fugitives. A twenty-minute chase ended in the shooting of a gunman identified as a fugitive Black Panther. Hours later police seized Jeff Jones and his wife, among the last identified leaders of the Weather Underground to escape capture in the eleven-year search for members of the group.

In April 1984, Kathy Boudin pleaded guilty to murder and robbery charges in the Brink's holdup. "I feel terrible about the lives that were lost," she told the judge. "I have led a life of commitment to political principles, and I think I can be true to those principles without engaging in violent acts." The judge sentenced Boudin to ten years to life in prison. She will be eligible for parole in the year 2001, when she will be fifty-eight years old. Four other defendants in the Brink's case were convicted of murder, robbery, and other charges and sentenced to seventy-five years to life in prison. Altogether, ten terrorists were convicted of involvement in the failed robbery and related crimes. The Brink's incident and its aftermath appear to have closed the books on the Weather Underground.

TERRORISM IN THE 1980s
Between 1980 and 1986 terrorist incidents in the United States numbered no more than fifty a year, an almost negligible number when compared with the nation's twenty-one thousand murders committed annually. Yet those few acts confirm the resilience of U.S. terrorists. Although the Black Liberation Army and the Weather Underground have been noticeably silent, recent bombings have led some law enforcement officers to suspect that remnants of these groups have formed or joined new terrorist organizations. At least one of these, the May 19th Communist Organization, is known to be a spin-off of the Weather Underground.

Between 1984 and 1985, groups calling themselves the United Freedom Front, the Armed Resistance Unit, and the Revolutionary Fighting Group claimed responsibility for bombings in New York City and Washington, D.C. The targets included branch offices of International Business Machines Company, Motorola, Inc., and the FBI, as well as a U.S. Navy officers' club and the Senate wing of the U.S. Capitol. The Senate majority leader said that "grievous injury and perhaps loss of life" would have resulted if the Senate had been in session when the bomb exploded. Kenneth Walton, the FBI's deputy assistant director and head of an antiterrorist task force in New York, speculated that the groups responsible for the bombings were linked to the Black Liberation Army: "They use the same kind of rhetoric, the same kind of weapons, and their symbolic targets are similar."

Perhaps the most active, most persistent of U.S. terrorist groups has been the FALN. Its violent campaign for Puerto Rican independence began in the 1940s with attacks on President Harry Truman and members of the House of Representatives. Between 1974 and 1985, the group was responsible for nearly 150 bombings and incendiary attacks. In 1979 FALN leader William Morales, charged with killing a Mexican policeman, escaped from custody. Federal prosecutors say that accomplices to his escape were the Black Liberation Army and the May 19th Communist Organization.

Morales's escape was further confirmation that U.S. terrorists have established some form of a coordinating body. A former terrorist who became an FBI informer has testified that in 1976 terrorists representing various organizations formed a group called "the family." According to the same source, the family still exists and consists of more than 200 cells around the country, each with five to twenty-five black, Hispanic, and white members. If these assertions are true, then the potential for terrorism in the United States cannot be underestimated. For that reason, the FBI alone has assigned five hundred agents to the antiterrorist activities.

CHAPTER
SEVEN

RED ARMY,
RED BRIGADES

TERRORISM IN
WESTERN EUROPE

*We regarded ourselves as the fifth
column of the Third World, and cared
very little about the German workers.
For us, in fact, the German workers
were part and parcel of the capitalist
system—people who by now already get
a share of the loot. The workers can
only be so well off in our country
because the masses in the Third World
are so badly off.*

Michael Baumann,
a member of the
Baader-Meinhof gang

*I am used to being thought a monster
to be struggled against. That doesn't
bother me. I am a combatant. When
one is a revolutionary one needs to
accept the idea of bestowing death and
receiving it. To kill or be killed is the
simplest thing in the world.*

Renato Curcio, co-founder
of the Red Brigades

The story of West Germany's Baader-Meinhof gang begins with the story of two German radicals: Ulrike Meinhof and Bernd Andreas Baader. Baader was born in Munich on May 6, 1943. His father, a professor of history, served in the German army and was killed in Russia during World War II. Andreas was raised in a small flat in Munich by his mother, an aunt, and a grandmother. His mother worked as a typist and secretary. He did fairly well in school, but because of discipline problems, was expelled from high school, and was unable to continue his education. He was an avid reader, deeply en-grossed in the philosophy of Nietzsche and Sartre and in the novels of Balzac. He enjoyed American movies, and friends say he affected the mannerisms of Humphrey Bogart.

Baader moved to West Berlin, where he attended art school for a time, and worked briefly as a reporter for a daily news-paper. He met Gudrun Ensslin, the daughter of a Protestant clergyman and a political activist who would change the direc-tion of his life. These were the days in 1968 when protests and massive demonstrations against American policy in Vietnam were frequent events in West German cities. At one of these demonstrations, called to protest a visit by the shah of Iran, a German student was killed by a police bullet. His death was the spark that ignited radical violence.

Under Gudrun Ensslin's influence, Andreas Baader became a militant. Together, on April 2, 1968, they fire-bombed two of Frankfurt's largest department stores. As the bombs exploded just before mignight. Ensslin and Baader joined the crowd that watched the blaze. They were arrested, and then tried, convicted, and sentenced to three-year prison terms. But Ensslin escaped and went underground. Even so, she disguised herself and visited Baader in late April 1970. In May Baader was visited five times by West Germany's most famous left-wing journalist, Ulrike Meinhof.

ULRIKE MEINHOF

Meinhof was born in Oldenburg in 1934, the years after Hitler came to power. Her father, a lecturer at the College of Art in nearby Weimar, died when she was six. She was reared by her mother and her mother's closest friend, Renate Riemeck, a professor and a leader of the "ban-the-bomb" movement. In her teens, Ulrike herself became active in the movement.

At the university, she completed her studies in sociology and philosophy with distinction. Soon after, in 1961, she married Klaus Reiner Röhl, the publisher of *Konkret*, a magazine then emerging as the voice of the student left. A year later, she gave birth to twin daughters. As editor of *Konkret*, she became famous and influential. Her columns were recognized even by opponents as good political journalism. She and her husband lived in a fashionable suburb and socialized with celebrities such as Günter Grass. She appeared on television talk shows.

But a friend says, "She knew she was living a lie—cavorting with the rich and yearning to liberate the poor." In 1968, after the failure of the student revolts, Meinhof sued her husband for a divorce and, taking the twins with her, moved to West Berlin. There she wrote a series of articles on the plight of children raised in state institutions. But increasingly, reform seemed to her an unpromising method of change.

It was this evolution that led Meinhof to express admiration for those who fire-bombed the Frankfurt department stores; that led her to visit Baader in May 1970; and that caused her to write a letter to prison authorities from a fictitious publisher stating that Baader had been commissioned to write a book for them. She requested that Baader be allowed to research his manuscript in the library of the Institute for Social Questions in a suburb of West Berlin. Permission was granted, and Andreas Baader arrived at the Institute on the morning of May 14, 1970, to begin his research.

GOING UNDERGROUND

That morning in May 1970 marked the official birth of the Baader-Meinhof gang. Ulrike Meinhof had arrived just after eight o'clock, settling herself in the Institute's reading room. Baader arrived in a prison van at nine-thirty, accompanied by guards. Shortly before eleven, the doorbell rang, and the librarian admitted two young women who said they wanted to do research for an essay on juvenile delinquency.

Minutes later, the doorbell rang again. This time the caller was a tall man in a hooded mask, who shot the head librarian in the stomach. In the reading room, the two women removed guns from their briefcases and aimed them at the guards. Baader and Meinhof escaped through a window, covered by the three other terrorists. A waiting car sped them to a "safe house." Now they were underground in West Berlin. For the next eighteen months, they were the object of West Germany's largest manhunt, which involved five thousand police.

Soon after the escape, Baader, Meinhof, Ensslin, and several others made their way across the border to East Germany. From there they flew on the East German airline Interflug to Jordan. In Jordan and Lebanon, they were trained by Palestinian terrorists in marksmanship, the use of explosives, and terrorist tactics. At the end of August they returned to West Germany. They devised code names, and acquired weapons and false ID cards. And following the example of Marighella, they robbed banks to finance their operations.

On September 29, 1970, the gang robbed three West Berlin banks simultaneously, coming away with about $60,000. In January 1971 they raided two banks in the small town of Kassel and got away with more than $30,000. But the actions exacted a high toll—by the middle of the year, the group had lost fifteen of its original twenty-two members, several having been killed. Baader, Meinhof, Ensslin, and a small core held out. In December they robbed another bank and killed another policeman. Despite dragnets, wiretappings, and interrogations, none of the gang's inner circle was caught.

They were quiet for a few months when, in May 1972, they exploded a series of fifteen bombs throughout West Germany. The first three destroyed the officers' club of the U.S. Fifth Army Corps in Frankfurt. Other bombs were targeted for the

U.S. Army's European Supreme Headquarters in Heidelberg, the Augsburg police headquarters, a publishing company, and the car of the wife of the judge who signed arrest warrants for members of the gang. Five persons, including four American servicemen, were killed in these May 1972 bombings.

In targeting Americans for their attacks, the gang was acting on its belief that "American imperialism is a paper tiger . . . that can ultimately be defeated because its forces are fragmented." Terrorism, they believed, would ignite "the class struggle." Meinhof stated in a 1972 Manifesto:

> We mean by this that the guerrillas will expand, will gain a foothold; that the development of class struggle will itself carry the concept through; that the guerrilla idea developed by Mao, Fidel, Ché, Giap, Marighella, is a good idea; that it can no longer be swept under the table.

Critics described the Baader-Meinhof gang as anarchist. And it is true that they had read and admired the writings of Bakunin and Nechaev. But anarchists officially disowned the group. The terrorists considered themselves Marxists, but East Germany's official Communist party condemned them: "The Baaders and the Meinhofs are not revolutionaries or Marxist–Leninists. They are disappointed middle-class children without revolutionary discipline and without fundamental political knowledge."

They dreamed of creating a leftist utopia. Instead they created a rightist reaction that threatened Germany's democratic institutions. The woman who had helped raise Meinhof, Renate Riemeck, pleaded with Ulrike Meinhof to surrender: "I don't feel qualified to give you advice, but I do beg you not to keep giving the rightists more ammunition. They are on the march everywhere."

THE CAPTURE
The end came soon and very quickly. On June 1, 1972, Baader was captured in a spectacular ambush by sharpshooters, highway patrols, and helicopters. A week later Ensslin was arrested in a Hamburg boutique. In her handbag police discovered a gun, a forged ID card, and newspaper clippings of

Baader's arrest. A week after Ensslin's arrest, Meinhof was seized after a radical young teacher with whom she was hiding informed on her. She struggled with police, calling them "pigs," but was subdued. In her luggage, police found three 9-millimeter pistols, a submachine gun, two hand grenades, a gift-wrapped homemade bomb, and thousands of cartridges of ammunition.

Baader, Meinhof, and the others remained in prison for several years, awaiting trial. Prosecutors had difficulty fixing responsibility on individuals for acts that were collectively planned and executed. And with the help of some of Germany's ablest lawyers, the defendants seized upon every legal tactic and ploy that might improve their position.

In prison, the gang caused authorities as much trouble as any prisoners in history. Various escape plans were discovered, and threats were received. As a result, the prisoners were classified extreme security risks and confined in isolation with few privileges. (Among the few visitors they were allowed was Baader's idol, Jean-Paul Sartre.) The prisoners managed to communicate with each other through an ingenious system they had devised. And from his prison cell, Baader may very well have taken part in planning the bombings, the hijackings, and kidnappings that were to come. "As long as Andreas Baader lives," said a defector from the gang, "the terror will never end."

And the terror continued, engineered by a "second generation" of terrorists—remnants of the Baader-Meinhof group and others, who identified themselves as the Red Army Faction (RAF). In November 1974, in retaliation for the death of an RAF hunger striker in prison, the terrorists assassinated Dr. Gunter von Drenkmann, chief judge of West Berlin. In February 1975, Peter Lorenz, leader of West Berlin's Christian Democratic party, was kidnapped and released in return for five prisoners, who were flown out of the country. In April an attack on the German embassy in Stockholm caused four deaths.

THE TRIAL AND ITS TOLL

The first Baader-Meinhof trial had ended in a mistrial. The second trial, which began in May 1975, was expected to last two years. It became the most widely followed judicial proceeding in Germany since the trials of Nazi war criminals in the late 1940s. A new courthouse built at a cost of $10 million had a built-in antiaircraft defense system designed to repulse helicopter attacks. Judges, the accused, and witnesses sat behind bulletproof glass. There were five hundred guards with cars and tanks.

As the trial progressed, a sensationalistic right-wing press inflamed German opinion, which became obsessed with terrorism. The word "sympathizer" became a dirty word. One newspaper editor wrote, "The sympathizer is no better than the murderer." In West Berlin, an art teacher's loyalty was questioned because previously she had belonged to an art society to which one of the Baader-Meinhof lawyers belonged. Novelist Günter Grass was suspected of being a sympathizer for his attacks on the right-wing press, and because he wore a beard. Said Manfred Rommel, the mayor of Stuttgart, "A sympathizer became anyone who criticized how democracy was being run in Germany."

New laws enacted by the German Parliament stated, among other things, that defendants could not have more than three defense attorneys of their own choice. Defense attorneys could be excluded from trials on *suspicion* of participating in the criminal acts of their clients. Other new laws required mandatory loyalty screenings for prospective government employees, and defined "defaming the state" as a misdemeanor punishable by imprisonment. The Conservative party called for increased wiretapping and demanded that anyone who walked in a demonstration that led to violence be arrested. As the trial dragged into its second year, German society veered to the right, and the fear that Renate Riemeck had expressed to Ulrike Meinhof was confirmed: the Baader-Meinhof gang had given the rightists "more ammunition."

EXIT MEINHOF
After forty-four months in prison, Meinhof no doubt ceased caring. She had spent 231 days in solitary confinement in a small cell in which everything was painted a luminous white; where the neon lights were never extinguished; where the only window was covered so that the sky could not be seen; where she could hear no voices, no sounds—nothing. Friends

believed that the eight months of solitary confinement had deranged her. Whatever the reason, on May 9, 1976, Ulrike Meinhof hanged herself from a crossbar of her window. She left no farewell note. Neither her foster mother nor her daughters were at the Protestant cemetery of the Church of the Holy Trinity in West Berlin, where she was buried. But four thousand other mourners were there. They carried banners that said: "Justice Terror" and "Murder in Jail," and leaflets that described Ulrike Meinhof's suicide as "her last combat measure."

But Meinhof's suicide was not the gang's last combat measure—not by far. On April 7, 1977, West Germany's attorney general—the person in charge of the entire Baader-Meinhof prosecution—was murdered. The Red Army Faction claimed responsibility the next day, signing its open letter "Kommando Ulrike Meinhof." On July 30, 1977, the president of West Germany's second largest bank was shot and murdered in Frankfurt by three young women, among them one of his daughter's close friends. They had appeared at his apartment on his birthday with a bouquet of red roses. Leaving the flowers scattered on his body, the women disappeared, and widespread searches produced nothing. In the meantime, in April 1977, Baader and Ensslin had received life sentences, which they were to serve in the huge new Stammheim prison in Stuttgart, a facility built with terrorists in mind.

AN UNEXPECTED
TURN OF EVENTS
In September 1977 a bizarre and spectacular operation began that raised Baader's and Ensslin's hopes for escape. On September 5, Hans Martin Schleyer, one of Germany's most powerful industrialists and a former Nazi SS officer, was being driven to his Cologne apartment in his Mercedes-Benz, followed by another car with three bodyguards. As the two cars drove down a one-way street, a woman suddenly pushed a baby carriage into the road. As Schleyer's driver swerved and braked, the guards' car smashed into his Mercedes. A Volkswagen bus drove up and five terrorists jumped out, spraying the guards' car with machine-gun fire that killed all three men. Another terrorist shot Schleyer's driver in the head. Schleyer

was bundled into the bus, which drove off. Altogether the operation had taken ninety seconds, and the only witness was a ten-year-old boy who thought they were shooting a film.

Less than twenty-four hours later, authorities received a color Polaroid photograph of Schleyer—a "mug shot" in which Schleyer held a cardboard sign that said "Prisoner of the RAF." With the picture came a letter from Schleyer in which he wrote: "I'm told that further attempts to find me or any delays in complying with their demands will be bad for me." The kidnappers demanded the immediate release of Baader, Ensslin, and nine other RAF members, each of whom was to be provided with $43,000.

As time passed, the police, the government, and the public became increasingly frustrated. Successive deadlines set by the terrorists came and passed—partly because their letters sometimes arrived after deadlines had expired, partly because the government was stalling for time. Neither side would compromise, and finally there was silence and grim anticipation.

CLIMAX AT MOGADISHU

And then the episode took still another bizarre turn. On the afternoon of October 13, 1977, Lufthansa flight 181 took off from Palma, Mallorca, bound for Frankfurt with eighty-two passengers and a crew of five. Forty minutes after takeoff, two male passengers produced pistols from their boots, and two women brandished grenades. While the women guarded the passengers, the men stormed the flight deck of the Boeing 737, commandeering the plane. The leader, who called himself Mahmoud, demanded the release of all political prisoners in Germany. If his demands were not met by noon on Sunday— within seventy-two hours—the terrorists would blow up the plane and its passengers.

For the next seventy-two hours, the plane flew aimlessly around the Middle East. After several stops for refueling, it landed at Aden, on the Persian Gulf, on October 16. There Mahmoud executed the pilot in an outburst of rage, leaving the corpse on the floor of the passenger cabin. "After that," said one of the passengers, "we didn't have much hope." The following morning, the plane was flown by the copilot to Mogadishu, the capital of Somalia.

Unknown to the terrorists, they were followed by another plane carrying thirty members of an elite West German commando unit. Mahmoud had extended the deadline by ten and a half hours, the time he reckoned it would take to fly the freed prisoners from Stuttgart to Mogadishu. But in the middle of the night, on October 18, with terrorists and their hostages sealed in the Lufthansa jet, the plane carrying the German commandos landed. Within minutes, simultaneous explosions ripped open the front and rear doors of the hijacked airplane. Sharpshooters fired numbing grenades that stun, blind, and deafen those within the target area for six seconds. Within those six seconds, commandos killed three of the terrorists and seriously wounded the fourth. Seven minutes later, the passengers were safely in the terminal.

"THAT'S IMPOSSIBLE!"

At 7:30 the next morning—less than eight hours after Chancellor Schmidt received the good news from Mogadishu—the guards on the seventh floor of Stammheim Prison unlocked Andreas Baader's cell. They found him dead, shot in the neck with a pistol which lay next to his body. Gudrun Ensslin was also found dead, hanging from one of the bars of her cell window by a piece of electrical wire. Another member of the group, Jan Carl Raspe, had been shot just above the right ear; he died in the prison hospital. And another terrorist, Irmgard Möller, had been stabbed several times in the chest, but survived. When Chancellor Schmidt heard of the deaths, he turned to an aide and shouted, "But that's impossible!"

A team of pathologists from Switzerland, Austria, and Belgium conducted autopsies and agreed that Baader, Ensslin, and Raspe had committed suicide. Several years later, Irmgard Möller said that she had no recollection of having tried to kill herself. Yet other evidence supported the suicide story. Two secret holes had been found in the cells of Baader and Raspe: one contained elements of a communications system that, when connected to cells of a thermostat, formed an effective telegraph. In addition, authorities found dynamite, two pistols, and a transistor radio.

Later on the same day that the suicides were revealed, October 19, a Paris newspaper received a message saying,

"After 43 days we have put an end to the miserable and corrupt existence of Schleyer. . . . His death does not measure up to our grief and anger over the slaughter at Mogadishu and Stammheim. Schmidt can take delivery in the rue Charles Péguy in Mulhouse. The battle has just begun." In Mulhouse, just across the German border, French police opened the trunk of a green Audi and found Schleyer's body. He had been shot three times in the head—apparently as soon as news of the Mogadishu operation reached the kidnappers.

In the intensified manhunt that followed, the West German government filled the streets with police, monitored all cross-country traffic, and covered walls with nearly four million posters. Berlin was transformed into an armed camp. But Schleyer's killers were not captured.

Since 1977 the hard core of the Red Army Faction has gone through a reconsolidation. In the 1980s, strengthened by new recruits, the RAF has become gradually more troublesome, targeting its attacks on U.S. military bases in West Germany. In 1981, it bombed Ramstein Air Base, wounding eighteen persons. In August 1982 the group planted a car bomb outside the headquarters building of the Rhein-Main Air Base, killing two Americans and wounding about twenty others, including West Germans.

In November 1985, thirty-four persons were wounded when a bomb planted in a car was detonated just outside a crowded American military complex in northern Frankfurt. The RAF and the French terror ring Direct Action jointly claimed responsibility for the bombing. This attack prompted West German Federal Prosecutor Kurt Rebmann to describe the RAF as the "most dangerous organization in West Germany," and its potential for terror as "undiminished and acute." Subsequent events have confirmed the soundness of his evaluation. Between December 1984 and August 1985 the RAF and allied gangs carried out 156 bombing and arson attacks.

Recent actions by the RAF reveal that today's terrorists, unlike those of the 1970s, are inclined to direct their violence at ordinary people, and not just at the political, economic, or military leaders targeted in the past. Moreover, the joint claim of responsibility for the Frankfurt bombing by the RAF and

Direct Action suggests that European terrorist organizations are beginning to cooperate, especially in confronting what they perceive as the international threat of organizations such as NATO. Frequent bank robberies by the terrorists indicate that the groups are well funded. Whether the growing wave of anti-American, antinuclear sentiment in Western Europe will contribute to their resurgence remains to be seen.

ITALY'S RED BRIGADES
Of the many terrorist groups that have plagued Italy since the late 1960s, the most notorious is *Brigate Rosse*, or the Red Brigades, which stands out for the breadth, efficiency, and brutality of its operations. The Red Brigades was formed in 1970 by Renato Curcio, his wife Margarita Cagol, and several others. Most of the members had belonged originally to communist youth organizations, and later to the Italian Communist party, which they finally rejected. They consider themselves "true" communists, as opposed to the "bourgeois" party. They aim to force the government to take such repressive measures that workers will rise up and overthrow it.

By 1975 the Red Brigades was believed to consist of four hundred to five hundred full-time members, who received regular salaries of about $400 a month. In addition to the hard core of underground terrorists, a hundred or so members lived seemingly normal lives, going underground only occasionally to lend support. The group can also claim thousands of sympathizers, including professors, journalists, and even wealthy industrialists. The fact that police reports were found in captured hideouts suggests that the Red Brigades infiltrated the police and probably also the judiciary.

The Red Brigades began its operations with acts of sabotage in the factories of Milan and Genoa. Its tactics escalated to include kidnapping; maiming, including "knee-capping," or shooting victims in the legs; and, finally, murder. These acts provoked equally vicious counterterrorism by fascist terrorists who planted bombs at antifascist rallies, killing eight persons in 1974; and who exploded a bomb on an express train that same year, killing twelve.

In 1974 it seemed that the Red Brigades had been broken, when an informant led police to Renato Curcio and other key members of the group. Then, in June 1975, police killed Margarita Cagol Curcio in a shoot-out at a farmhouse used as a secret prison for kidnapped victims. Even so, terrorist incidents did not diminish, numbering 702 in 1975 alone. In many cases, police could not be certain of the perpetrators, although the Red Brigades was thought to be responsible for most of the incidents.

The trial of Curcio and the others was delayed for several years, regularly postponed because of violent attacks on those involved, including lawyers, witnesses, and judges. The trial finally began in March 1978, with the government determined to show that it had the power to enforce basic laws and bring terrorists to justice. For its part, the Red Brigades promised to strike at the heart of the state. A week later, it made good on its promise.

THE KIDNAPPING
OF ALDO MORO

On the morning of March 16, 1978, former prime minister Aldo Moro, the leader of Italy's Christian Democratic party, left his home in the Monte Mario district of Rome. Like all important Italian political figures, he was provided with a bodyguard and a motor escort with additional guards. As Moro's Fiat 130 and his escort car, with three agents, entered the narrow Via Licino Calvo, a Fiat 128 with diplomatic plates preceded them. Suddenly it slammed to a stop. The escort car smashed into Moro's Fiat, causing it to smash into the Fiat 128. Instantly a man and a woman jumped from the first car, rushed to Moro's car, and emptied submachine guns into the front seat, killing Moro's bodyguard and his driver. At the same time, four men dressed in Alitalia pilot uniforms, who had been waiting on the sidewalk, sprayed the escort car with gunfire, killing the three agents. Moro was shoved into a waiting blue Fiat 132 that had been used to block traffic in the cross street. In a convoy with two other cars, the Fiat 132 drove off with Aldo Moro.

Within an hour police had assigned three thousand men to the case. Within twenty-four hours there were three thousand searches; there were roadblocks; there were appeals. But the police found nothing. On March 18 the Red Brigades issued a communiqué claiming responsibility for the kidnapping and saying that Moro would undergo a "people's trial." A photograph of Moro was enclosed, showing him in front of the red star flag of the Red Brigades. Despite the kidnapping, the government announced that the trial of Curcio and the others would proceed in Turin.

The trial proceeded, and the government refused to negotiate with the terrorists for Moro's release. As time passed, the crisis heightened. On April 24, a new Red Brigades communiqué demanded the release of Curcio and the others on trial in Turin; otherwise, it said, Moro would be executed. A letter from Moro was enclosed, and in it he wrote, "We are almost at zero hour, seconds rather than minutes from the end." Then there followed eleven days of silence.

On May 5 a Red Brigades' communiqué announced, "We have concluded the battle begun on March 16 by carrying out the sentence to which Aldo Moro has been condemned." Two days later Moro's farewell letter to his wife arrived: "They have told me they are going to kill me in a little while. I kiss you for the last time." On May 9, after fifty-four days, Moro's body was found in the luggage compartment of a Renault R-4 parked in the center of Rome. He had been shot ten times in the chest.

On June 25, 1978, sentences were handed down in the trial at Turin. Renato Curcio and other founders of the Red Brigades were convicted of subversion and given prison terms of thirteen to fifteen years. But terrorism continued after the sentences, as it had during the trial. In 1978 alone there were sixteen murders and twenty-five maimings—a level sustained over the next two years. In 1981 police arrested Mario Moretti, a thirty-five-year-old electronics expert from a devout Roman Catholic family. He was identified as the leader in the Moro kidnapping and murder, as well as chief of the Red Brigades after the capture of Curcio. With Moretti's capture, police claimed in August 1981 that they had "decapitated" the Red Brigades, as well as Front Line, Italy's second most powerful terrorist group. But events that followed called that claim in question.

THE DOZIER KIDNAPPING
In December 1981 came the Red Brigades' most ambitious operation since the abduction and killing of Aldo Moro. This

time its victim was U.S. Brigadier General James L. Dozier, a senior staff officer at the NATO headquarters for southern Europe in Verona. On December 17 four terrorists disguised as plumbers overpowered the general in his apartment, bound and gagged his wife, and carried him off in a trunk.

With the Dozier kidnapping, Italy's largest police operation began, surpassing in scope even the long, unsuccessful search for Moro. This time the effort was rewarded with success. Acting on information provided by an informer. Italian anti-terrorist forces traced the kidnappers to an apartment in Padua. They burst into the apartment and liberated the general un-harmed, just as one of the terrorists was putting a gun to his head. A search of the apartment yielded five machine-pistols, seven hand grenades, six packages of plastic explosives, various kinds of ammunition, about $20,000 in *lire*, false identity documents, and detailed files on regional political leaders and other prominent figures.

For the Italians the capture of Dozier's kidnappers was a great morale booster. For the Red Brigades it was a disaster. Two of the five terrorists captured in the Dozier abduction were linked to Moro's slaying. Some of the captured terrorists impli-cated others, thanks to a new law that permitted plea bargain-ing. Altogether, more than 140 members of the Red Brigades and Front Line were arrested. In March 1982 General Dozier's abductors were sentenced to prison terms ranging from two years and two months, to twenty-seven years. Following the Dozier incident, the terrorist threat in Italy receded.

Giovanni Spadolini, who was Italy's prime minister at the time, said: "We were looking at the last offensive of the Red Brigades. . . . We beat them with our own forces and within our laws. The political effect has been to strengthen the country. It put borders on the left. The Communist party took part in the common struggle. Now the situation is very different. Terrorist cells used to be mixed with political groups. That is no longer true. The terrorists are isolated—outside the national conscience."

Although the threat posed by the Red Brigades now seems manageable, Italian authorities worry about those who have found sanctuaries elsewhere, mainly in France, where they may have taken part in the operations of Direct Action. One person who will never underestimate the group's potential is James Dozier. Asked for his impression of the group after forty-two days as a captive, the general replied: "They're a bunch of dedicated people. They're smart. They believe in what they're doing; and they're very serious about it."

CHAPTER EIGHT

SECRET ARMIES

TERRORISM IN IRELAND

*Mullaghmore, Ireland, Aug. 27.
Earl Mountbatten of Burma, one of
the heroes of modern British history,
was killed today when his fishing boat
was blown up in the sea, apparently by
terrorists of the Irish Republican Army.*

*The 79-year-old World War II hero died
instantly in the explosion, which occurred
a quarter mile off the coast, near his
summer home here in the northwest of
Ireland. A 14-year-old grandson and a
15-year-old passenger were also killed and
four other passengers in the 29-foot boat,
including a daughter, Lady Brabourne,
were seriously injured.*

*The explosion this morning reverberated
like thunder through this peaceful little
seaside village. A witness who saw it
from the shore said, "The boat was there
one minute and the next minute it was like
a lot of matchsticks floating on the water."*

*In Belfast, Northern Ireland, the Provisional
wing of the Irish Republican Army issued a
statement taking responsibility for the killing,
which it called "an execution," and vowed to
continue the "noble struggle to drive the
British intruders out of our native land."*

New York Times, *August 28, 1979*

Under the terms of the Anglo-Irish Treaty of 1921, the six Protestant countries of Northern Ireland, which are called Ulster, remained part of the United Kingdom of Great Britain and Northern Ireland. The twenty-six Catholic counties in the south of Ireland became the Irish Free State, a self-governing British dominion. In 1949 the Irish Free State became the Irish Republic, severing all ties with the British Commonwealth.

The moderate wing of the Irish Republican Army, which had led the struggle against Britain, was willing to accept the treaty, even though it denied the nationalist objective of Irish unity. With other moderates, Sean MacBride renounced the path of violence and entered politics. He became one of Ireland's most distinguished trial lawyers, the founder of a political party, and minister for External Affairs. He then held several high international posts, including assistant secretary general of the United Nations. From 1961 until 1974 Mac-Bride was chairman of Amnesty International, an organization devoted to securing the release of prisoners of conscience worldwide. In 1974 MacBride was awarded the Nobel Peace Prize.

Not all of the Irish nationalists followed MacBride's example. The more radical members of the IRA remained underground, unreconciled to the existence of two Irelands. In the late 1930s, IRA terrorists carried out a futile bombing campaign in England. Between 1956 and 1962, the IRA carried on a border campaign in Ireland, attacking customs posts, police barracks, and communications in Ulster. But they failed to rally popular support for their violence. Outlawed by the governments in London, Belfast, and Dublin, and weakened by internal conflict and futile campaigns, the IRA seemed finished.

ULSTER FOR
THE PROTESTANTS

In the meantime, the Protestants of Ulster, a two-to-one majority over the Catholics, had created "a Protestant state for a Protestant people." Ulster's parliament, called Stormont, legalized political and social injustices against the Catholics in voting, housing, employment, and social welfare. Glad to be rid of the Irish problem for the first time in centuries, the British looked the other way.

In 1968 a small but vocal civil rights movement was formed by Catholics in Ulster. In 1969, when Catholics protested discrimination with peace marches and demonstrations, Protestant extremists responded with gang attacks and arson in Belfast's Catholic slums. When Northern Ireland's police lost control of the situation, British troops arrived to protect the Catholic minority. But gradually the British came to be perceived with hostility by Catholics and Protestants alike.

At a secret meeting in Dublin in late 1969, the IRA tried to reach a consensus on its response to Protestant action in the North. Two-thirds of the delegates favored a political approach to the problem. But the other third argued for a renewal of violence. At this meeting the IRA split into two factions. The moderates became known as the Official IRA, or the "Officials," and the more militant group became known as the Provisional IRA, the "Provisionals," or "Provos." Though differing on methods, both groups share a single objective—a united, socialist Irish republic.

THE NEW FACE
OF IRISH TERRORISM

The Provisional IRA launched its terrorist campaign in 1970, with tactics that were strikingly different from those of the original IRA in the 1920s. For Tom Barry, a legendary fighter of the 1920s, terrorism was a highly selective form of violence. He is famous for the remark, "There are no bad shots at ten-yards range." But the Provisionals opted for a strategy of random terrorism. More often than not, their victims are both

[104]

innocent and unknown to them. Sean MacBride has remarked: "The things which are done today by what you call terrorist movements—take the IRA—would not have been dreamt of in the IRA I knew twenty or thirty years ago."

The Provos aimed to produce a breakdown of law and order, forcing Britain to abolish the Ulster government and set up direct rule over Northern Ireland from London. They began their campaign with bombings in the major cities of Belfast and Londonderry. The violence led to riots and burnings in both cities. In August 1971, when the British authorized the Ulster government to intern suspected terrorists without trial,. Northern Ireland was swept by savage and bloody violence. Supported by Catholic mobs, terrorists turned Belfast and Londonderry into blazing combat zones.

In January 1972, British paratroopers killed fourteen civilians during a Londonderry civil rights rally, further alienating Catholics. In Dublin, two nights later, a mob burned down the British Embassy while Irish police stood idly by. In March 1972, as the situation steadily worsened, England imposed direct rule over Northern Ireland. One objective of the IRA had been achieved.

THE CAMPAIGN ESCALATES
In 1973 the Provisional IRA carried its terrorist campaign to England, hoping to fuel England's desire to withdraw from Ulster altogether, letting the Protestants fend for themselves. There were bombings in stores and public buildings, on streets, and at railroad stations. In June 1974, a bomb exploded in Westminster Hall, the nine-hundred-year-old section of the British Parliament. The next month, another bomb exploded in an armory of the Tower of London, killing one person and injuring forty-two, mostly tourists. The wide publicity given the bombings was a lesson for the IRA. As their spokesperson stated, "Last year taught us that in publicity terms one bomb in Oxford Street [in London] is worth ten in Belfast. It is not a lesson we are likely to forget."

The bombings in England reached a frightening level on the evening of November 21, 1974, when powerful explosions destroyed two crowded pubs in Birmingham, killing 21 persons and injuring 184. Public outrage forced the Provos to modify their tactics, and in 1975 they attacked only elite hotels, clubs, and restaurants, killing fewer, wealthier, but no less innocent, victims.

There were terrorist attacks in the United States and the Irish Republic, as well as in Ulster and England. In 1973 an exploding letter bomb tore off the hand of a secretary in the British Embassy in Washington. In May 1974, 28 persons died and 130 were injured when three bombs exploded in the center of Dublin during the peak rush hour. One year later the publisher-editor of the *Guinness Book of Records*, Ross McWhirter, was shot dead. He had offered a $100,000 reward for ideas to combat terrorism. In 1976 Britain's ambassador to the Irish Republic, Christopher Ewart-Biggs, and his secretary were killed when their car passed over a road mine. In 1979 Lord Louis Mountbatten and members of his party were killed by a bomb in their fishing boat off the shore of Ireland.

Since the early 1980s the frequency of IRA terrorism has diminished. The organization has lost people at a significant rate, both in battle and through arrest. Many IRA leaders are dead or in prison. In the summer of 1981, IRA prisoners at Maze Prison outside Belfast went on a hunger strike, demanding that they be treated as prisoners of war. Prime Minister Margaret Thatcher resisted their demand, arguing that to grant the prisoners any status other than that of common criminal would be to recognize their cause. Ten hunger strikers died before the strike ended in October 1981.

For a while the IRA was penetrated by British intelligence. As a result, the organization was reorganized, becoming more cellular and more difficult to penetrate. But newer members have tended to be young and inexperienced, faring badly in battle with British army units. For that reason, IRA terrorists have begun selecting "softer" targets—off-duty members of the Ulster constabulary, for example.

Yet one of the group's most daring acts came in October 1984, when IRA terrorists nearly succeeded in assassinating Prime Minister Thatcher. Despite the tightest security measures of the British police, the terrorists were able to conceal a bomb in the hotel occupied by the prime minister at a party convention. The bomb exploded directly beneath the prime minister's room, collapsing three floors of the hotel. But it exploded two minutes before Thatcher entered her room. After the near miss, the IRA announced, "Today we were unlucky, but, remember, we only have to be lucky once."

A NEW SITUATION

In 1981, the prime ministers of Britain and the Irish Republic began a series of meetings that were intended to improve the Irish situation. Those meetings led to the signing of a pact between the two nations in November 1985. The pact gives the Irish Republic a voice in the running of Northern Ireland, whose status as part of Britain would change only with the consent of the population.

By giving Dublin a say in the affairs of Northern Ireland, the two prime ministers hoped to break the cycle of violence that has caused 2,450 Roman Catholic and Protestant deaths since 1969. If the agreement is to succeed, however, Thatcher's government must convince Protestant hard-liners that it does not jeopardize Northern Ireland's ties with Great Britain. For his part, the Irish prime minister must reassure Irish critics who fear that the accord sets back the prospects of Irish re-unification.

After the signing of the pact, the Ulster Freedom Fighters, a Protestant paramilitary group, announced that anyone who collaborates with the Anglo-Irish consulting body established by the pact will be "classified as legitimate targets for assassination." Several days later, tens of thousands of Protestants turned out for a huge rally in Belfast to show their opposition to giving Dublin any say in controlling their affairs.

Despite the opposition, both the British and Irish parliaments approved the agreement by comfortable margins. In Northern Ireland, the Reverend Ian Paisley, a Protestant hard-liner, vowed to fight the accord constitutionally. "But in battered Ulster," wrote *Newsweek* reporter David Newell, "no one ever counts the gunmen out, and last week few seemed willing to wager much that the battle over the Anglo-Irish accord would stay limited to the courtroom." Just one minute into 1986, IRA terrorists killed two policemen and wounded a third in an ambush. The IRA said that the attack marked the opening of a new campaign against British security forces.

Protestant and Catholic terrorists alike are mistrustful of

a political settlement. Both groups fear being "sold out." The Protestants warn the British that abandoning Ulster would be no different from abandoning Yorkshire. The IRA insists that in Ireland as a whole, the Protestants are a minority and should give in or get out.

Britain, too, has very litle room to maneuver. Britain cannot be seen to give in to terrorism; it cannot persuade the Protestants to make significant concessions; it cannot withdraw its army for fear the Protestants would annihilate the Catholics in Northern Ireland, sparking a Civil war extending to all Ireland. The British say, moreover, that they cannot pull out of their own territory, for the same demands might then be made in Scotland or Wales.

Ireland's nationality and religious problems seem to defy solution. Only one member of the government of the Irish Republic, Conor Cruise O'Brien, has ever challenged the extreme nationalist position publicly. Irish unity, O'Brien has argued, may be neither inevitable nor logical. Yet the Provisional IRA and its supporters will accept nothing less than unity. The solutions they have so far proposed, said O'Brien, are "alternative routes to the cemetery."

In 1916 William Butler Yeats glorified the "terrible beauty" unleashed by the Easter Rebellion. But in the same poem, he foresaw the likely result of fanaticism, as well as the hopelessness that is prevalent today in Ireland:

Too long a sacrifice
Can make a stone of the heart.
O when may it suffice?
That is Heaven's part, our part
To murmur name upon name,
As a mother names her child
When sleep at last has come
On limbs that had run wild.
What is it but nightfall?
No, no, not night but death;
Was it needless death after all?

CHAPTER NINE

THE OTHER
PALESTINIANS

TERRORISM
IN THE
MIDDLE EAST

*Despair will drive the Palestinians
increasingly to acts that will consume
the world's tranquillity.*

*Yasir Arafat,
founder of Fatah;
chairman of the Palestine
Liberation Organization*

*In the war against Israel and the
Western imperialists, there are no
innocents. You are either for us
or against us.*

*George Habash,
founder of the
Popular Front for the
Liberation of Palestine*

A major event in the history of Arab nationalism was the birth of the state of Israel on May 14, 1948. The founding of Israel by the Palestinian Jews was consistent with a United Nations resolution that recommended the partition of Palestine into a Jewish state, an Arab state, and the international city of Jerusalem.

On the day following Israel's declaration of independence, the armies of Jordan, Egypt, Syria, Lebanon and Iraq, supported by contingents from Saudi Arabia and the Yemen, invaded the new state to "drive the Jews into the sea." As the fighting raged, some seven-hundred thousand Palestinian Arabs fled to neighboring Arab countries, which encouraged them to do so and promised them a swift return with their victorious armies.

Despite the odds, the Israelis crushed the Arabs, occupying territory intended for the never proclaimed Arab state. Jordan and Egypt occupied the remaining fragments of Palestine—the West Bank of the River Jordan and the Gaza Strip. The United Nations Relief and Works Agency, UNRWA, was set up to care for the Palestinians. Refugee camps were opened for them for what everyone believed would be a temporary stay. But they were still there in 1967, when Israel defeated the Arabs in another war, when seizing the West Bank and Gaza. Another two hundred thousand Palestinians swelled the population of the camps.

By most estimates some four million Arabs consider themselves Palestinians today. According to the United Nations, more than a half million of them live in UN-sponsored camps in Syria, Lebanon, Jordan and the Israeli-occupied West Bank and Gaza. Another 1.2 million Palestinians live outside the camps in these same countries. The rest are scattered throughout the Middle East, Europe, and the United States.

Israel insists that the Palestinians were incited to leave their lands by the Arab states. The Arabs say the Palestinians were evicted at bayonet point. The Israelis and others argue that the Palestinians could have been resettled years ago in Gaza and on the West Bank. But the Arabs opposed such a solution, unwilling to accept the existence of Israel, and preferring to use the camps to pressure world opinion. So the camps remain today—a reminder of the stateless condition of the Palestinian Arabs, and an important recruiting ground for the fedayeen. The fedayeen—from the Arabic word for "he who sacrifices himself"—are Arab terrorists.

THE EMERGENCE
OF ARAFAT
Among the Arabs who fled Palestine in 1948 was Yasir Arafat. Arafat was born in 1928 in Jerusalem, the son of a well-to-do textile merchant. Through his mother he was related to the openly pro-Nazi Moslem leader, Haf Amin al-Husseini, who was exiled by the British to Cairo during World War II. During the war, Arafat's father and older brother were both active in an anti-Zionist paramilitary force called Holy Struggle.

In 1951 Arafat entered the University of Cairo, where he studied engineering and became active in politics, widening his contacts with militant Palestinians in exile. During these years he and some friends formed the group that later became known as Fatah, which means "conquest."

Early in 1956, Arafat was elected chairman of the Palestinian Student Union. Later that same year he traveled to Prague as a delegate to a communist-sponsored international student conference. In October 1956, when British, French, and Israeli forces fought Egypt along the Suez Canal, Arafat served as a lieutenant in the Egyptian army.

After the war, Arafat moved to Kuwait, on the Persian Gulf, first working the Department of Public Works, then starting a contracting firm of his own. He extended his network of contacts with Palestinians throughout the Persian Gulf, winning wider recognition and support for Fatah. Early in the 1960s he raised the money required to form the first military unit of Fatah, which would "blaze armed revolution inside the occupied territory" of Israel.

As late as 1965, Arafat was making the rounds of Beirut's newspaper offices, seeking publicity for his group. But after Israel overwhelmingly defeated the Arabs in the Six-Day War of 1967, Fatah came into its own. With the destruction of the Arab armies, Fatah's strategy of guerrilla warfare and terrorism was the one promising anti-Zionist strategy left.

By 1969 Fatah's membership was estimated at nearly ten thousand. In that same year, at a congress of Palestinian militants in Cairo, Arafat and his group assumed control of the Palestinian Liberation Organization, or PLO, whose 350 members represent various groups of Palestinians, including trade unionists, women, refugees, and the fedayeen. The PLO acts as a cover organization for at least nine groups of terrorists, who run the ideological gamut from extreme left to extreme right; from Marxist-Leninist to Islamic. In addition to Fatah, they include the Popular Front for the Liberation of Palestine; the Palestine Liberation Front; the Popular Struggle Front; the pro-Libyan Popular Front for the Liberation of Palestine— General Command; the pro-Syrian As Saiqa; the pro-Iraq Arab Liberation Front; and the pro-Soviet Democatic Front for the Liberation of Palestine.

FATAH: THEORY
AND PRACTICE
Fatah has kept its political program deliberately vague—in a way that could appeal to both left and right. Fatah's emphasis is nationalistic. It sees Israel as an artificial state inserted within Palestine by the Western powers. After the Jews are defeated, says Fatah, they will discard their Zionist ideals and take their place in a secular, binational Palestine.

Frantz Fanon had a strong influence on the founders of Fatah, which once published a condensed version of Fanon's book, *The Wretched of the Earth*. Fatah's manifestos have emphasized Fanon's notion of "liberating violence." According to one such statement, "The colonized will be liberated from violence by violence." And according to another, "Blazing our

[113]

armed revolution within the occupied territory [Israel] is a healing medicine for all our people's diseases."

Fatah's efforts to organize a rural guerrilla movement in Israel in 1967 failed. A campaign of terrorism in the refugee camps of Gaza in 1968 and 1969 also had failed. Fatah was at a disadvantage because its camps were outside Israel, in neighboring Arab states. And even there, Fatah was not always secure. In Jordan it had become a state within a state, threatening King Hussein. In September 1970—which came to be known as "Black September"—Hussein's Bedouin troops attacked Fatah's camps, decimating the fedayeen and driving them from Jordan.

From that event emerged a terrorist group called Black September. Israeli and other intelligence specialists believe that Black September was controlled by the PLO and Fatah— by Arafat, that is—and that it was used to perform particularly gruesome acts with which Fatah could not associate itself. Other analysts believe that Black September consisted of a group of particularly dangerous militants—supported by Libya, perhaps—over whom the PLO and Fatah had no control. The first act for which Black September claimed responsibility was the assassination of Jordan's prime minister in the lobby of the Cairo Sheraton Hotel in November 1971. This was Fatah's revenge for being driven from Jordan in September. Yet to come were the spectacularly shocking acts aimed at Israel.

MUNICH

One such act was committed at the 1972 Munich Olympics and witnessed by as many as five hundred million people around the world. Eight Black September terrorists penetrated the living quarters of the Israeli athletes, killing two of them and capturing nine others. The terrorists demanded an escape plane, and the West German government complied. At the airport, German security forces tried to free the hostages before they boarded the plane, but the operation collapsed into a chaos of gunfire and grenade explosions. All nine of the Israelis were slain, together with five of the terrorists and a German policeman. Black September had made its point: there could be no peace, not even at the Olympics, so long as the Palestinians were ignored.

Other Black September atrocities followed. In March 1973, Black Septembrists seized the American embassy in Khartoum, killing one Belgian and two American diplomats. In August 1973 there was a raid on the departure lounge at Athens airport that killed three tourists and injured many more. In December 1973 there was another airport raid, this time in Rome, and thirty-two travelers were killed. Arafat suggested that it was virtually impossible to stop the activities of Black September. Nevertheless, he forbade air piracy in 1974, arguing that it was counterproductive to the Palestinian cause. After 1974 little was heard of Black September, while Fatah launched terrorist acts against Israel from its new sanctuary in neighboring Lebanon.

GEORGE HABASH
AND PFLP

If Fatah is the preeminent group among fedayeen organizations, credit for being the most innovative must go to the Popular Front for the Liberation of Palestine, or the PFLP, and its leader, George Habash. It was Habash and the PFLP who first enlisted foreign nationals in their cause, forming a kind of international brigade of terrorists. And it was they who took the first step away from the Fatah's futile guerrilla strategy to spectacular deeds against "soft" targets such as airlines. Publicity was a key consideration in PFLP's choice of tactics. "Let me explain," wrote Habash:

The attacks of the Popular Front are based on quality, not quantity. We believe that to kill a Jew far from the battlefield has more of an effect than killing 100 of them in battle. It attracts more attention. When we set fire to a store in London, those few flames are worth the burning down of two kibbutzim.

PFLP's campaign of sky piracy opened in July 1968, when three terrorists—two Palestinians and one Syrian—seized an El Al airliner en route from Italy to Israel and forced the pilot to fly to Algeria. There Algerian president Boumedienne took over, demanding the release of certain Arab prisoners held by Israel in return for twenty-one Israeli passengers and the Israeli crew. Reluctantly, Israel complied.

The cycle of violence continued with attacks on other El Al planes at airports, more hijackings, and attacks on El Al offices in Brussels and Athens. Airlines from nations friendly to Israel were also attacked. In August 1969 a TWA aircraft was hijacked to Damascus and blown up on the ground. Soon after this incident, PFLP terrorists planted a bomb on a Swissair jet bound for Israel. The plane exploded in flight, killing forty-seven passengers and crew members, including sixteen Israelis.

In September 1970 PFLP attack teams in Europe took command of four New York-bound jets soon after takeoff. These included a Pan Am 747, a Swissair DC-8, a TWA 707, and a BOAC VC-10. The Pan Am plane was diverted to Beirut where nine terrorists came aboard and wired the first-class cabin with explosives. The plane was then flown to Cairo. There its passengers and crew were removed, and it was blown up—in protest against Egypt's acceptance of an American peace initiative.

The other jets, with 751 hostages, were directed to Dawson Field, an old unused British airstrip north of Amman, Jordan. From there the PFLP demanded the release of terrorists held by West Germany, Switzerland, Great Britain, and Israel. Israel rejected all concessions, instead seizing 450 Arabs in the occupied zones of West Jordan and Gaza as "counter-hostages." The Swiss, German, and British governments yielded, surrendering their convicted or otherwise legally held prisoners in exchange for the release of the 751 hostages. The terrorists then blew up the three giant planes, and had themselves photographed on the debris, waving and shouting revolutionary slogans before a television audience of millions.

PFLP's next gruesome act came in May 1972, when terrorists at Lod Airport near Tel Aviv fired into the crowded waiting room, killing twenty-eight people. At Lod the terrorists were Japanese, recruited and trained through agents in North Korea, supported by funds from West Germany, given final training in Syria and Lebanon, armed in Italy, and sent by the PFLP to a destination unknown to them in advance.

Despite Arafat's condemnation of air piracy in 1974, PFLP persisted in its strategy. In June 1976 three men and one woman hijacked a giant Air France plane on a Tel Aviv–Paris flight, with 244 passengers and a twelve-member crew. Two of the terrorists were Arabs; the third, Wilfried Boese, was a member of West Germany's Baader-Meinhof gang, and the woman was Turkish. They forced the plane to fly to Uganda's Entebbe Airport, where they were warmly received by dictator Idi Amin, and joined by four more Arab terrorists. At Entebbe, the terrorists released 148 of their hostages, holding only those they believed to be Jews. In return for their release, the terrorists demanded the release of fifty-three terrorists held in Israel, Kenya, and Europe.

The Israeli government agreed to negotiate, while secretly it prepared a raid to rescue the hostages. Israeli planes with specially trained troops, including doctors and nurses, flew the 2,620 miles to Uganda, swooping down on Entebbe at midnight on July 3. They killed seven hijackers and some twenty Ugandan soldiers, rescuing 103 hostages and the crew. Three hostages and one Israeli officer were killed during the battle, and soon after, enraged Ugandan toughs murdered an elderly British-Jewish woman who had been moved from the airport to a hospital before the rescue.

Another Arab terrorist group embraced by the PLO is the Popular Democratic Front for the Liberation of Palestine, or PDFLP, whose leadership broke away from the PFLP in 1969, branding Habash and his group "bourgeois." The PDFLP boastfully claimed responsibility for the slaughter at Ma'alot in May 1974. In that incident, three PDFLP terrorists entered Israel from Lebanon, seized a schoolhouse and ninety teenaged hostages, and demanded the release of terrorists held in Israeli prisons. Saying that "we cannot wage war over the head of our children," Prime Minister Golda Meir agreed to negotiate. The prisoners had already been taken from their cells when negotiations went awry and Israeli troops opened fire in an effort to free the children. The terrorists then began to shoot the children, killing twenty-six and wounding many others.

TERRORISM VS. DIPLOMACY

In 1974 the PLO was recognized by Arab heads of state as "the sole legitimate representative of the Palestinian people." Later that same year, Arafat was given a reception at the United Nations, a ceremony normally reserved for heads of state. Since then the PLO has been allowed to open offices in some fifty nations, and it has been granted observer status by five United Nations agencies. These and other events were highlights of a broad diplomatic offensive that Arafat believed would strengthen the PLO's position in future negotiations.

Arafat and his followers in Fatah have always believed—in theory, at least—that diplomacy might help lead to the creation of a Palestinian state. But other, more radical, factions within the PLO vehemently oppose negotiation and compromise altogether. As Arafat waged his diplomatic offensive, he alienated these fanatics and undermined his authority within the PLO. Then, in 1982, Israel invaded Lebanon, determined to drive the PLO from that country. The Israeli invasion further undermined Arafat's authority, perhaps fatally.

As a result of Israel's military action, about twelve thousand fighters were driven from Lebanon, dispersing to nine Arab countries around the Mediterranean and on the Persian Gulf. PLO headquarters were relocated from Beirut to Tunis and Damascus, Syria. In these circumstances, Arafat's control over the PLO has been slipping. In the absence of progress, the more radical strand in the Palestinian movement has come to the fore, personified by the terrorist leader Abu Nidal. Before 1985 Abu Nidal was a fringe figure in Palestinian politics, since 1985 the fringe has started to become the center.

Ariel Merari, of Tel Aviv University's Center of Strategic Studies, has followed the evolution of Abu Nidal and concludes: "When you look at his whole career, Abu Nidal makes the infamous terrorist Carlos look like a Boy Scout. As far as Palestinian terrorism goes, he definitely holds all the records. He has no equals."

ABU NIDAL

Abu Nidal was born Sabri al-Banna in British-controlled Palestine. Some sources say that he was born in 1935; others say 1943. The youngest of a wealthy merchant's seven sons, he attended an upper-class school in Jerusalem. During Israel's war of independence in 1948, Abu Nidal's parents left Jaffa and settled in what was then Jordan and is now the Israeli-occupied West Bank. After graduating from a Jordanian high school, Abu Nidal was a schoolteacher for a while, before joining his brother in the construction trade in Saudi Arabia. He joined Arafat's Fatah in 1959, the year that it was founded in Kuwait.

Abu Nidal broke with Arafat in 1974, believing Arafat's diplomatic offensive to be a betrayal of Palestinian interests. After the break, he became a "subcontractor" for Iraq, Syria, and Libya, carrying out murders and others terrorist acts related to inter-Arab feuds. In return, his clients gave him money and weapons for his private war with Arafat. In 1974 Abu Nidal sent a "hit team" to Damascus to assassinate Arafat. The team was captured, however, and tried by the PLO. In the trial Abu Nidal was sentenced in absentia to death for attempting to kill the PLO chairman.

Until recently, Abu Nidal's group concentrated on attacking Jordanian interests, seeking revenge for Jordan's backing of Arafat. In 1985 the group gained international notoriety with a series of attacks, most of them in Europe. In July the group was probably responsible for the bombing of two restaurants in Kuwait, killing eight and injuring almost ninety. In August and September the group bombed two hotels in Athens, injuring thirty-two persons. In September they bombed a British Air office and a café in Rome, injuring nearly sixty persons. In late November the group hijacked an Egyptair passenger plane in an action that ultimately cost the lives of fifty-nine passengers. On December 27, it conducted simultaneous attacks on airline offices in Rome and Vienna, leaving more than a dozen dead, including five Americans.

According to a report on Abu Nidal issued by the U.S. Department of State, the group claimed responsibility for more than sixty terrorist attacks between 1978 and 1985—at least thirty of them since the beginning of 1984. Those attacks have taken place in more than twenty countries on three continents. According to a senior PLO leader, Abu Nidal receives support from a surprising variety of sources, including Iran, conservative Arab regimes, and other radical terrorist movements. In an interview with the editor of a Kuwaiti newspaper, Abu Nidal said, "Give me $400 million and I'll change the face of the Middle East in five years."

For Abu Nidal, experts say, violence is an end in itself. He has no known ideology or plan of action for the Palestinian people. He gave up working for a Palestinian state long ago, and now advocates perpetual war with Israel. His politics is the politics of revenge. When one of Abu Nidal's men who had been captured in the December 1985 raid on Viennna's airport was asked what his mission had been, he replied, "To kill Israelis."

Israeli philosopher David Hartman has written that Abu Nidal and his followers believe that "the anger and frustration of the deprived give them the right to destroy all moral boundaries," even to shoot up an airport and kill everyone in sight. What's more disturbing is the fact that Abu Nidal can draw followers in increasing numbers from among the young Palestinians living in refugee shanty towns. Arab analysts in Beirut have said that if the Palestinian deadlock continues, Abu Nidal's outlook will come to dominate the Palestinian movement in the late 1980s.

CHAPTER TEN

THE WEB OF TERRORISM

Terrorism is a growth industry.

Ambassador Robert B. Oakley,
Office for Counter-Terrorism
and Emergency Planning,
U.S. Department of State

A few days before Christmas, 1975, a group of young people, one wearing a beret and an open white trench coat, entered the headquarters of the Organization of Petroleum Exporting Countries (OPEC) in Vienna. Reporters in the lobby noticed that they all carried sports bags and that one of the group was a young woman in a maxi dress with a gray wool cap over her head. They did not look like OPEC people and they were not.

The man in the white coat was Ilich Ramirez Sanchez, better known as "Carlos-the-Jackal," who has been called "the most wanted terrorist in the world." Born in Venezuela, Carlos studied in Moscow and acquired international connections as a playboy in London before turning to terrorism. Others in the group of six terrorists included two Germans—members of the June 2 Movement—two Palestinians, and one who could have been German or Latin American.

Four minutes after entering the building, Carlos drew a submachine gun from under his trench coat and demanded, "Where's the conference room?" Within the next few minutes, as they shot their way into the conference room, the terrorists killed two Arab staff members of OPEC and an Austrian policeman. One of the terrorists, the German Hans-Joachim Klein, was seriously wounded. But the terrorists had captured the oil ministers of eleven oil-exporting countries, including Sheikh Ahmed Zaki Yamani of Saudi Arabia.

Speaking Arabic, Spanish, German, and English, the captors read their prisoners a lengthy statement demanding that the world's oil be denied to the West and that war be declared on Israel immediately. The terrorists demanded and got a jetliner from Austria's Chancellor Bruno Kreisky. They ordered the crew to fly them and some fifty prisoners first to Algeria, then to Libya, and back to Algeria. In the cockpit of the commandeered plane, Carlos told the Austrian captain, "Violence is the only language the Western democracies can understand."

Gradually releasing all but the most important of the oil ministers, the terrorists were said to be planning to kill Sheikh Yamani and Iran's oil minister, Jamshid Amuzegar. But the Saudis, Iranians, and Austrians agreed to pay a huge ransom, and the Austrians transferred a sum estimated from between $5 million and $50 million from a Swiss bank to Aden. On December 30, the terrorists departed for "a friendly Arab country," probably Libya.

TERRORIST NETWORKS

The raid on OPEC and many other acts of terrorism in the 1960s and 1970s indicated a growing solidarity among terrorists around the world. The roots of what some have called an "international terrorist network" can be traced to the Tricontinental Congress held in Havana in January 1966. The more than five hundred delegates to the Congress called for close cooperation among "socialist countries"—the Soviet Union and its satellites—and "national liberation movements." The resolutions passed by the delegates covered not only third-world groups, but also "democratic worker and student movements" of Western Europe and North America. Their objective, the delegates agreed, was to devise "a global revolutionary strategy to counter the global strategy of American imperialism."

Encounters among terrorists multiplied in the years that followed the Havana Congress. From their exile in Algiers, Eldridge Cleaver and other Black Panthers visited Peking, Hanoi, and North Korea. Black Panthers in the United States opened a channel of communication to members of the Québec Liberation Front. In Germany in 1974, Spanish Basque terrorists had formal meetings with representatives of the Tupamaros. At about the same time, the IRA established links to France's Front for the Liberation of Brittany, the Free Welsh Army, and German and Italian terrorists. And German and Italian terrorists met with Swiss anarchists.

In 1975 French police discovered that Carlos-the-Jackal ran a Paris clearinghouse for terrorist movements that included the Tupamaros, the Québec Liberation Front, the IRA, the Baader-Meinhof group, Japan's United Red Army, Yugoslavia's Croatian separatists, the Turkish People's Liberation Army, and Lebanon's Palestinians. Carlos escaped capture in a shoot-out in which he killed two French police officers.

By the 1980s the working relationship among terrorists had become a closer one. In Europe, there have been more frequent signs of cooperation among the German, French. Italian, and Belgian groups, for example. In June 1984 Belgian terrorists known as the Fighting Communist Cells stole more than 800 kilos of plastic explosives from a quarry near Brussels. Six bombs subsequently used in separate terrorist acts in West Germany, France, and Belgium were found to have been made from this material, and the bombs had identical triggering devices.

In January 1985, General René Audran, who directed French arms sales abroad, was murdered while parking his car in a suburb of Paris. Ten days earlier, Direct Action and the Red Army Faction had issued a joint communiqué claiming they had formed "a political-military front" in Western Europe to attack NATO targets. Audran was such a symbol.

FINANCING TERRORISM

Nineteenth-century terrorist movements were run on a shoestring. The People's Will got the little money it needed from well-to-do members or sympathizers. The anarchists were poor and had no significant source of support. The Irish Revolutionary Brotherhood was founded in 1858 with $400 received from the United States. The Irgun received financial support from Jews in the United States and also engaged in "expropriations."

Contemporary terrorism, by contrast, is big business. The income of the PLO is as great as that of poorer Arab countries, with payments by the Arab oil producers ranging from $150 to $200 million a year. Officials of the organization are paid $5,000 or more a month, and given automobiles. In Latin America, the Argentine ERP and the Montoneros amassed millions of dollars through bank robberies and extortion. Ransom money collected by Argentine terrorists was traced to other groups in both Latin America and Europe. Terrorists in Ulster, the Philippines, Eritrea, Sardinia, Corsica, Thailand, and elsewhere have received generous contributions from more prosperous groups. The IRA, the PLO, and other groups receive generous contributions from sympathizers in the United States.

Libya, whose leader Colonel Qaddafi vows to "export revolution to every country that opposes us," has allocated some $73 million to terrorist group in recent years. According to Iranian sources, Libya disbursed more than $1 million to Iranian terrorists in 1976, and increased its contribution dramatically during the 1978–79 struggle that overthrew the shah. Libya has offered special bonuses for successful operations. For the murder of the eleven Israeli athletes at Munich in 1972, Libya donated $5 million. Between $1 and $2 million were paid to Carlos for the OPEC raid. The German participant in that raid, Hans Joachim Klein, reportedly collected $100,00 for his role. According to Egyptian sources, Libya offered $16 million to the PFLP for the assassination of President Sadat several years before he was killed by Egyptian terrorists in 1981.

For the most part, the experts do not believe that the Soviet Union or the Eastern-bloc countries provide outright financial support to terrorists. An official of the U.S. State Department has said, "The terrorists wouldn't have to rob banks if they were getting help from the East." Reinhard Rupprecht, a senior official of the West German government and a respected authority on terrorism, says flatly, "There is no evidence of direct support from Eastern Europe."

TRAINING AND
COMBAT MATERIEL

Fidel Castro has operated schools for guerrillas and terrorists since 1961, first accepting recruits from Latin America and Africa, and later, from Palestine, Europe, and North America. In 1967, one year after the Tricontinental Congress in Havana, more than a dozen training camps for guerrillas and terrorists from all over the world were opened in Cuba under the direction of Colonel Vadim Kotchergin of the Soviet security services, or KGB. Colonel Kotchergin's camps marked a major commitment by the Soviet Union to the terrorist network, and enhanced Castro's capabilities. Among those who received training in Cuban camps were Weather Underground members Bernardine Dohrn and Mark Rudd.

Training camps for terrorists have also been located at different times in Algeria, Iraq, Jordan, Lebanon, Libya, and South Yemen. Some of these camps have been controlled by governments, and others by various PLO groups, especially Fatah and PFLP. Libya administers camps where hundreds of terrorists are trained each year. For very advanced training, Libya sends its own and other volunteers to Syria and Algeria.

Thousands of Arab and foreign terrorists from some fifteen countries have passed through Middle East camps. Carlos, who joined the PFLP in 1970, received his indoctrination and training in a Jordanian camp, where he later sent other terrorists for training in sabotage, hijacking, and assassination. Japanese United Red Army recruits also began training at PFLP bases in Jordan in 1970. Members of the Baader-Meinhof gang and other German terrorists received training in the early 1970s at Fatah camps in Lebanon and Syria. Other European terrorists trained in the Middle East have included members of Italian, Irish, Dutch, and Norwegian groups.

In the procurement of combat materiel, cooperation among terrorists and foreign support have also played a role. In the mid-1970s, modern military equipment, including portable antitank launchers and antiaircraft missiles, began to reach underground movements. The major sources of these weapons appear to be the Soviet Union and Czechoslovakia, although the equipment is actually procured from various Arab countries and the PLO. For example, in 1975, Libya signed a $2 billion arms deal with the Soviet Union. Some of the weapons eventually were sold or given to various terrorist groups by the Libyan government.

Palestinian groups frequently serve as intermediaries in the supply of weapons. In 1977 five tons of PLO hardware—mortars, rocket launchers, automatic weapons, and explosives—were intercepted in Belgium. The arms, intended for the IRA, were hidden in electrical transformers being shipped from Cyprus to the Irish Republic. Early in 1978 the IRA received a new supply of weapons from the Middle East, including American M-60 machine guns that had been purchased from the United States by various Arab states. Later in 1978, the Argentine Montoneros received Soviet-made rockets from Palestinian terrorists.

The flow of military supplies goes both ways. In 1978 the Baader-Meinhof gang gave the Provisional IRA three sets of American electronic night vision binoculars, which can detect infrared ray equipment used in after-dark surveillance. The binoculars had been stolen by the gang in a raid on a U.S. Army depot in West Germany. At about the same time, the Baader-Meinhof gang gave American M-26 hand grenades and other weapons to the Japanese United Red Army and to Carlos. Some of these weapons were traced to a villa outside Paris, which was shared by the PFLP, Turkish terrorists, and an Algerian leftist group.

All such evidence further confirms a continuing and perhaps growing degree of cooperation among the world's terrorists since the 1960s. Indeed, this has been one of the most important developments in the history of contemporary terrorism. It explains how an operation such as the OPEC kidnapping can be planned in the Middle East by a Venezuelan, financed by the Libyan government, and carried out in Vienna by German, Palestinian, and Latin American terrorists using American and Czech arms.

WHO SPONSORS TERROR?

Early in his administration, President Reagan implied that the Soviet Union was training, funding, and equipping international terrorists. But the administration's views on the Soviet role in terrorism were immediately challenged.

American intelligence officials said there was little evidence to back up assertions of direct Soviet involvement in international terrorism, though there is evidence of indirect links. Intelligence officials acknowledged that in the 1960s the Russians set up training and support centers in the Soviet Union and other countries to train guerrillas for what the Soviet Union calls "wars of national liberation."

Later some of these centers outside the Soviet Union were used by the Libyans, the Cubans, the PLO, and others to train terrorists of the Baader-Meinhof gang, the Red Brigades, and the United Red Army. The Soviet Union knew about these activities, and there is no evidence that it tried to block them. As William E. Colby, the former director of the Central Intelligence Agency, has testified: "Given the fact that the Soviets set these centers in motion, they are not without responsibility, and there is no evidence of their urging restraint on the terrorists."

Yet there is also little evidence that the Soviet Union is directing international terrorism or any network of terrorist organizations as the administration has claimed. In reply to questions about Soviet-sponsored terrorism in the United States, F.B.I. Director William H. Webster said: "I cannot speak about activities abroad, but I can say that there is no real evidence of Soviet-sponsored terrorism within the United States." And in an article in the *Wall Street Journal*, Henry Rositzke, a former CIA analyst and specialist on the KGB, spoke out most candidly, challenging the logic of the administration's position:

> With all due respect for the KGB, no service can totally control and manipulate a dozen regimes and security services, including such men of spirit as Colonel Kaddafi and Fidel Castro. The training, funding, and equipping of global terrorism that Moscow is officially charged with . . . does not need the Kremlin. Oil dollars count today, not rubles. Small arms and explosives training is a simple two-week exercise. The required materiel (Soviet, American, Swiss) is available to all comers with cash.

TERRORISM VS. "WARS OF NATIONAL LIBERATION"

The attitude of current Soviet leaders toward terrorism is not unlike that of Marx, Engels, Lenin, Trotsky, Mao, and the other Marxists, who have applauded terrorism on occasion, but condemned it in principle. In recent years the Russians have supported a number of guerrilla movements, including those in the former Portuguese colonies of Angola, Mozambique, and Guinea-Bissau; and in Indochina, Zimbabwe, and Namibia. But the Russians have not supported such groups as the Baader-Meinhof gang, the Weather Underground, the Black Panthers, or the Red Brigades. And the Russians have denounced indiscriminate acts of terrorism such as airplane hijackings and the killing of diplomats.

The crucial distinction in the Soviet view is the distinction between terrorism and "wars of national liberation." For Moscow, terrorism as part of a "war of national liberation"—as in Vietnam, for example—is acceptable because it is presumed to have mass political support. But terrorism by groups with no popular support is regarded as irrational, and counterproductive to the cause of revolution.

Some policymakers, both in the United States and elsewhere, deny that such a distinction exists, equating terrorism with "wars of national liberation," and blaming the Soviet Union for both. Rositzke sees this tendency as "politically damaging":

> The two *are* different, both in definition and in practice, both in Moscow's eyes and, I hope, in Washington's. Anyone should hesitate to equate the "liberation" of South Vietnam and Angola with the actions of the Red Brigades in Italy. . . . The conspiracy thesis can only divert us from the long-term Soviet revolutionary threat. The main covert vehicle for expanding Soviet influence in the third world will continue to be wars of national liberation.

WHERE THINGS STAND

Since the late 1960s the Soviet Union has gradually disengaged itself from direct involvement with terrorist groups, letting Cuba and North Korea assume a larger share of the task. And Cuba's support for terrorists has become more selective, partly because of Soviet pressure, partly because the "revolutionary wave" of the 1960s has passed. Since then some Latin American terrorists have charged Cuba with betraying their cause, even though Castro continues to provide training, arms, and money to a select circle of terrorists.

For these and other reasons, it seems unlikely that there exists an international network of terrorists who take their orders from a single, clandestine source. Each terrorist group acts within very different national traditions which, in fact, discourage the development of a tightly knit network or conspiracy. Even so, the widening contacts among terrorist groups, their commitment to a shared revolutionary ideology, and their support by such governments as Libya could prove dangerous enough in the years to come.

PART III

THE
FUTURE
OF
TERRORISM

CHAPTER ELEVEN

TACKLING TERRORISM

If one comes to kill you,
make haste and kill him first.

A passage from the Talmud,
quoted by
Secretary of State
George P. Shultz, 1985

Striking a blow in a general
direction would be a terrorist act
in itself, one that could lead to
the killing and victimizing of
innocent people.

President
Ronald Reagan, 1985

In the first five months of 1985, some three hundred incidents of international terrorism resulted in the death of several hundred people. By summer 1985, international travel had become hazardous, especially for Americans, and President Reagan found himself in a quandry.

On June 14, TWA Flight 847, bound for Rome from Athens, was hijacked by terrorists of the Palestine Liberation Front. Flight 847's passengers, including thirty-nine Americans, were held hostage for seventeen days. One of those Americans, Robert Stethem, a nineteen-year-old seaman in the U.S. Navy, was tortured and killed by his captors.

On June 23, Air-India Flight 182, en route from Toronto to Bombay, crashed into the sea off Ireland, with a loss of more than 300 lives. Sikh terrorists claim to have planted a bomb aboard the plane to protest ongoing disputes with the government of India. On the same day as the Air India crash, a bomb planted in the cargo hold of a Canadian airliner exploded as the plane was being unloaded in Narita Airport in Japan, killing two persons. At about the same time a bomb explosion in Frankfurt's airport killed three travelers.

No terrorists were brought to justice on any of these occasions. In the TWA hostage incident—as in earlier acts in which Americans had been killed—President Reagan talked tough but failed to order the "swift and effective retribution" against terrorists that he had vowed in 1980, while campaigning for president. Instead, the president practiced restraint, and each incident served only to aggravate his frustration.

"This terrorism," the president said on one occasion, "this thing that is going on in the world, is the most frustrating thing to deal with. You know you want to say 'retaliate' when this is done, you want to get even . . . but you might be killing innocent people. . . ."

THE *ACHILLE LAURO* INCIDENT

Then, in October 1985, an incident occurred that gave the president the opportunity to deliver on his long-standing promise. In that month terrorists of the Palestine Liberation Front seized an Italian cruise ship called the *Achille Lauro* off Port Said, Egypt, holding its more than 400 passengers and crew as hostages. The gunmen killed a disabled, retired American passenger, Leon Klinghoffer, before agreeing with Egyptian President Mubarak to swap hostages for a promise of safe conduct to a secret destination.

On October 10, the hijackers of the *Achille Lauro* were put aboard an Egyptian 737 jetliner with two unidentified Palestinians for a flight to Tunis. There, presumably, they would be handed over to the PLO, which may have authorized the hijacking in the first place. Americans were enraged by the hijackers' release, demanding that they be apprehended and tried for the murder of Leon Klinghoffer.

Minutes after the Egyptian jetliner took off from Cairo, the USS *Saratoga*, cruising off the Albanian coast, launched four F-14 Tomcat fighters and one E-2C radar-reconnaissance plane. At almost the same moment, aboard *Air Force One*, President Reagan signed an order to the pilots of those planes to intercept the Egyptian 737.

Approaching a designated position over Egyptian territory, the American pilots identified the Air Egypt 737 and ordered it to proceed to Sigonella Naval Air Station in Sicily. Accepting the order, the Egyptian pilot followed the fighters to Sicily, where the hijackers were arrested by Italian authorities.

With one swift, stunning act, President Reagan had delivered the promised retribution, pleasing critics and supporters alike. At a press conference on the following day, the President said that terrorists had been put on notice that "you can run but you can't hide" from American justice. When he was asked if he would have gone so far as to order the hijacker's plane shot down, Reagan answered, "That's for them to go to bed every night wondering."

DECISION-MAKERS' DILEMMA

Because Americans have become the number one target of terrorism, the challenge of terrorism is especially urgent for the United States government. But despite the best intentions of several presidents, the United States has lacked an effective and consistent policy in its war against terrorism.

On the day that Ronald Reagan became president, fifty-two American hostages were released from their 444-day captivity in the United States Embassy in Tehran. The Iranian hostage crisis had haunted President Jimmy Carter during his campaign for reelection. His opponent, Ronald Reagan, had criticized his handling of the crisis, promising, if he were elected, to implement a policy of "swift and effective retribution."

Yet during the first five years of the Reagan administration, more than three hundred Americans were killed by terrorists. Not once was the United States able to use its elite Delta Force, a secret unit trained to deal with terrorists. Critics on the right condemned the president for his failure to take strong action, comparing him with President Carter.

Not long before the TWA hostage crisis, Secretary of State George P. Shultz had reaffirmed the Reagan administration's commitment to a tougher antiterrorist policy. In addressing a Jewish group in New York City, Shultz had declared: "Our goal must be to prevent and deter future terrorist acts, and experience has taught us over the years that one of the best deterrents to terrorism is the certainty that swift and sure measures will be taken against those who engage in it."

Shultz's speech was controversial because he had suggested that the United States should consider retaliating against terrorists even if innocent lives, including the lives of Americans, might be lost; and even if the United States retaliated "before each and every fact is known." Yet the seventeen-day ordeal of Flight 847's hostages ended without the promised retribution, reviving the policy debate in Washington. In the aftermath of that incident, President Reagan adopted a course frequently chosen by presidents for issues without answers. He appointed a commission, headed by Vice-President George Bush, and told it to produce an antiterrorism policy by the end of 1985. As of early 1986, the report had not been delivered.

QUESTIONS ABOUT
RETALIATION

Then came the *Achille Lauro* affair. While the capture of the *Achille Lauro* pirates boosted American morale, it did not signal a new American policy. When Abu Nidal's terrorists attacked the Vienna and Rome airports two months later, the United States made no effort to retaliate, and the policy debate began anew. This time, Secretary of Defense Caspar Weinberger openly challenged Secretary Shultz's position on retaliation.

Proposals for retaliation have always met with a mixed reaction, even within the Reagan administration. In Congress, members of the Senate Foreign Relations Committee have faulted the notion of retaliation on ethical grounds. One member has been quoted as saying, "You just don't talk about innocent people getting killed." In academic "think tanks," experts on terrorism have faulted the notion of retaliation on practical grounds, arguing that the United States lacks adequate intelligence to launch successful retaliatory strikes.

Critics of retaliation have argued, moreover, that it is harder to implement a retaliatory policy today than it was in the 1970s. In those days, most terrorist acts could be traced to groups that could be penetrated—the PLO, the Red Brigades, and so on. But in the 1980s, a growing number of incidents have been "state-sponsored" acts that can be traced to Iran, Syria, Libya, and other governments.

Critics of the Reagan administration's antiterror policy also insist that it is unwise to threaten retaliation before a terrorist act occurs. That is what President Reagan did during his first weeks in office, saying that the United States would never again be humiliated as it was in Iran. "That hasn't happened," notes Robert H. Kupperman of Georgetown University. "But when and if it does, you ought not to talk about it." Rather, says Kupperman, retaliation should be swift, covert, and a surprise to the terrorists.

To retaliate against terrorists, a government needs the means of retaliation. Like several other Western nations, the United States has created an elite antiterrorist corps, the Delta Force, to deal with terrorists directly. In several instances, these forces have been used with spectacular success—notably, in

Israel's attack on hijackers at Entebbe, and West Germany's attack at Mogadishu. But a would-be rescue mission intended by the U.S. to free the hostages in Iran was aborted, only embarrassing President Carter and aggravating his problems.

To bolster our means of effective retaliation in cases in which it might be appropriate, experts have suggested several measures. First, they say, we should deploy units of the Delta Force overseas, so they can be ordered into action without the loss of precious hours. Second, they say, we should bolster our covert intelligence capabilities. We can make all kinds of statements about preemptive strikes and retaliation, Robert Kupperman says, "but we really have to find the right terrorists."

A CONTROVERSIAL STRIKE

In addition to measures designed to bolster the retaliatory capability of the United States, other, more controversial, proposals have been offered. One of those proposals is to take direct military action or covert action against regimes that aid, abet, and sponsor terrorism, including Libya, Iran, and Syria. Covert actions would include political assassinations, which are currently forbidden by an executive order signed by President Reagan.

In 1986 the Reagan administration began to consider direct military action against Libya as mounting evidence linked Qaddafi to terrorist acts against Americans. For example, Qaddafi was implicated—at least indirectly—in Abu Nidal's attacks on the Rome and Vienna airports in December 1985.

Then—on April 5, 1986—a bomb exploded in a West Berlin nightclub frequented by American servicemen. An American soldier and a young Turkish woman were killed and 230 others wounded, among them some fifty Americans. In a televised press conference four days later, President Reagan indicated that Qaddafi was a suspect, and he hinted at more: "What we're trying to do is to find out who's responsible for a fine sergeant in our military dead and fifty young Americans lying in a hospital wounded because of that dastardly attack in West Berlin. And if there's identification enough to respond, then I think we respond. . . ."

By April 14, evidence gathered through intercepted telephone calls confirmed to President Reagan's satisfaction that the bombing had been carried out under direct orders of Libya. That evening, the president went on the air once again, this time to announce that air and naval forces of the United States had launched "a series of strikes against the headquarters, terrorist facilities and military assets that support Muammar Qaddafi's subversive activities. . . ."

Americans, by and large, supported the president's decision. In Congress Senator Richard Lugar, Republican of Indiana and chairman of the Foreign Relations Committee, said: "The United States has responded in an appropriate and a proportional manner to the terrorist attack on our citizens and soldiers in Berlin." But Senator Robert C. Byrd of West Virginia, the Democratic leader in the Senate, had serious reservations: "Are we going to do this again and again?" he asked. "I'm concerned there won't be any end to that approach."

The president and his team were convinced that the raid on Libya would deter terrorism in general, and state-sponsored terrorism in particular. Critics of the president's decision said that singling out Qaddafi would make it harder to fight other terrorists by absorbing energy that otherwise might be used for guarding embassies and airlines, gathering intelligence, and taking other preventive measures.

Even with the means and the determination to implement a retaliatory policy, retaliation has its limits. Military and paramilitary forces and actions can accomplish only so much against terrorists. For one thing, there are very few opportunities for military rescue missions. For another, retaliation is not always practical, even when the targets are military installations. Raids on Syria or Iran, for example, would be difficult because their primary targets are harder to reach. And attacking either of them would provoke the Soviet Union. For these and other reasons, many specialists argue, the U.S. government should give greater emphasis, and allot more money, to perventive measures.

THE CASE FOR PREVENTION
Preventive measures against terrorism tend to be overlooked or undervalued simply because their payoff is not apparent.

Yet, as Robert Kupperman has noted, the $100 million spent on security at the Los Angeles Olympic Games paid off. Several known terrorists were "interdicted," says Kupperman, before they could do any harm, and the games went on without incident.

Other promising, if costly, preventive measures include the appointment of more sky marshals and travel marshals; the beefing up of physical security at U.S. installations abroad; the refinement of intelligence operations, including better co-ordination among anti-terror units of the departments of State, Defense, and Justice and the Central Intelligence Agency; better surveillance of known terrorist groups; and the preparation of contingency plans for different kinds of terrorist acts in the United States, such as attacks against power and water systems.

On the diplomatic front, Kupperman and other terrorism experts have proposed making terrorism a subject of U.S.– Soviet negotiations. By doing so, we could minimize the chances that a terrorist act by a U.S. or Soviet surrogate could lead to a confrontation between the two superpowers. Other proposals include developing short-term economic sanctions to be used against countries that aid terrorists or fail to cooperate in the war on terrorism.

Finally, those concerned with fighting terrorism have proposed getting very tough on terrorist and would-be terrorist groups in the United States before they have the opportunity to organize effectively and carry out actions that could be costly. They have also proposed asking the television industry to adopt a code of self-restraint in covering terrorist activities, reasoning, as British Prime Minister Margaret Thatcher has said, that publicity is the oxygen of terrorism. These proposals are considered in the following chapter.

"TACTICAL TECHNOLOGY"
One area in which preventive measures hold great promise is air travel. By combining sophisticated technology with tight security procedures—what experts call "tactical technology"— airports could be made less inviting targets for terrorists than they are today.

An international airport is a crossroads that handles hundreds of flights each day to every part of the world. It is also a potential killing ground for terrorists. Beginning in 1969, there was an alarming rise in the number of hijacking attempts on aircraft. In that year, eighty-seven attempts were made at hijacking, including forty-seven aimed at American aircraft. In the following year, the attempts totaled eighty-three, including fifty-six aimed at American aircraft.

In no year since 1970 have there been fewer than eighteen hijacking attempts, or thirteen attempts aimed at the United States. Even though procedural changes in the handling of luggage and checking for explosives and weapons all make sense, they are at best stopgap measures. What really is needed is a terror-proof airport that would be radically different from the relatively open terminals of the present. Such an airport, ideally, would be isolated and surrounded by a guarded barbed-wire fence. Or, following the model of the airport in Amman, Jordan, it might be equipped with watchtowers and patrolled by military police.

Inside the terminal, passengers would be funneled through a few controlled checkpoints under constant surveillance by video cameras, guards on overhead catwalks, and armed security forces. The practice of allowing relatives and friends of passengers to accompany them to the boarding gate would end.

At the checkpoints, passengers would pass through metal detectors and be subject to body searches. Their passports would be checked against international criminal records. Carryon luggage would be x-rayed and searched under the supervision of armed law-enforcement officials. Luggage intended for the cargo hold would be matched against passengers, and no unidentified luggage would be loaded. Lockers, restrooms, restaurants, and other public areas would be eliminated or made more secure.

Even though some of these measures are years away, advanced technology is already used in some airports. British Aerospace has developed a $20-million cargo surveillance system that uses a mass spectrograph machine to analyze the air inside shipping containers and sound an alarm if it finds anything suspicious. The machine is sensitive enough to detect an unopened bottle of whiskey. The cargo then passes through a high-intensity X-ray machine that enhances the X-ray images and allows operators to compare them with images stored in a computer. More powerful X-ray machines would have foiled the hijacking of TWA Flight 847. In that incident, the terrorists smuggled weapons wrapped in fiberglass through the terminal's X-ray machines.

Some airports also subject cargo to air pressure changes, a precaution against bombs that use air pressure fuses. Engineers are exploring other technologies as well, including nuclear magnetic resonance, which is used by medical specialists to look inside the human body, and "thermal neutron activation," in which baggage is bombarded with radiation. And researchers hope to build a sniffer into an aircraft pressurization system that would warn the pilot during takeoff of any on-board explosives.

According to Brian M. Jenkins, a specialist on terrorism for the RAND Corporation, the central issue in preventing terrorism is that "terrorists can attack anything, while governments cannot protect every conceivable target against every possible kind of attack." Even though enhanced preventive measures will pay off, there must be a balance between security and personal freedom. If we turn airports and other facilities into armed camps, the terrorists will have won.

CHAPTER TWELVE

TERRORISM IN PRIME TIME

*Is it better for our cause to kill ten
of our enemies in a remote village where
this will not cause comment, or to kill one
man in Algiers where the American press
will get hold of the story the next day?*

*A leader of the
Algerian FLN, 1955*

*We just lost control of the medium; it was
theirs, not ours. We shifted shows in order
to meet their time-table. Our cameras had
to be in position to record each of the
released prisoners as they boarded the plane
to freedom, and our news coverage had to
include prepared statements at their dictate.
It was the gangsters who wrote the script
and programmed the mass media. . . .
Surely it must be the first recorded case of
how to hijack a national TV network.*

*West German
television producer,
describing TV coverage
of a hijacking, 1977*

On June 14, 1985, the newscasts of all three American television networks opened with the voice of John Testrake, captain of TWA Flight 847, speaking from his cockpit to the control tower of the Beirut International Airport:

They are beating the passengers. They are threatening to kill the passengers now. They are threatening to kill the passengers. We need fuel. We must get fuel.

With those words began the seventeen-day saga of TWA Flight 847, hijacked by Shi'ite Moslem terrorists as it left Athens for Rome. As the story unfolded, it came to dominate the attention of American television and the consciousness of millions of Americans.

Altogether, the three networks devoted more than sixty hours of broadcast time to the story. On the first day of the crisis alone, CBS offered special coverage on "The Morning News," "The Evening News," "Newsbreak," and in ten special reports, including a thirty-minute news special at 11:30 P.M.

In part, the emphasis the networks gave to the hostage story reflected their judgment that it was important. But this emphasis also reflected the competitive pressures to which the networks are subject—their drive to outdo one another in "the ratings." An ABC advertisement with newscaster David Hartman caught this competitive spirit well: "Wake up to the latest in the hostage ordeal on 'Good Morning America.'"

As a result of the media attention on the TWA hostage story, the Reagan administration found itself under strong public pressure to violate its policy of no negotiations. Because of the media's role, the outcome of the incident may have been decisively altered, and, as a result, questions about the proper role and responsibilities of television reporters covering terrorism were raised once again. Television, said its critics, is part of the terrorism problem.

DYNAMICS OF "TERRORVISION"

The players in the TWA hostage crisis included the terrorists, the leaders of the Amal militia who represented them in negotiations, the governments of the United States and Israel, the families of the hostages, and the television industry. The scenario of the crisis resembled that of many earlier crises in the age of "terrorvision."

At first the White House tried to hold down television coverage of the crisis, hoping to keep the incident in the background of public attention. The Reagan administration had always insisted that, in the long run, the best way to save the lives of hostages is not to negotiate with kidnappers at all. Giving in to their demands, this argument goes, will only give terrorists the incentive to kidnap others. The administration had long tried to win public support for this position. But as the TWA hostage incident came to dominate public attention, public opinion came to favor negotiations.

Three days into the crisis, the White House acknowledged that it could not control the situation. Lesley Stahl of CBS reported, "Administration officials say emotional pleas are making it more difficult to manage the crisis." At this point, some television journalists had begun to cast themselves in the role of diplomats. Said Stahl, "We [the television networks] are an instrument for the hostages. . . . We force the Administration to put their lives above policy." And ABC's David Hartman concluded a live interview with a spokesman for the Amal militia by asking, "Any final words to President Reagan this morning?"

Following the all-too-familiar logic of "terrorvision," the networks inevitably became the tool of two other players—the terrorists and the families of the hostages. The terrorists saw at the outset that American television could be used to carry their political message to the United States and the world.

Nabih Berri, the Shi'ite leader who served as the link between the hijackers and the U.S. government, wasted no time making an appeal through the media to Americans. He urged Americans to write to the president supporting the release of 700 Shi'ite prisoners in Israel.

At the same time, the families of the hostages discovered that they, too, could use the networks to further their own ends. Rejecting the administration's abstract aim of saving lives in the future, they pressured the president to negotiate with the terrorists now. One means of exerting pressure, as the brother of one hostage said, was "to keep public awareness as high as we can." For that reason, many members of the hostages' families made themselves available for interviews and appearances on talk shows as often as they were invited.

Writing in *TV Guide*, Sidney Diamond said that the networks had no choice but to allow themselves to be manipulated by the hijackers: "Both the hostage-takers and the hostage-sufferers had what the TV system needed—good pictures." Diamond continues: "[The images] of husbands and fathers expressing their desires for freedom, and wives and children reciprocating the anguish . . . were riveting. What viewer wouldn't feel 'those folks could be the people next door. They could be me.' The scenes were 'good TV.' "

DEFINING REALITY

Reflecting on the TWA hostage crisis and similar incidents, John Corry, television critic for the *New York Times*, wrote: "Television is used to change how the world thinks, or at least what it thinks about. We live in a time of instant communication; the world is a global village. Television is the universal hearth. Terrorists can speak to the world, and alter it, by capturing its cameras first."

As the TWA story progressed, the terrorists and the families of the hostages captured the cameras. By doing so, they won the power to define the problem and influence its solution. The situation became, less and less, the hijacking or the murder of a young American sailor among the passengers, and more and more, the need for negotiation. The central question became: What had to be done to set the hostages free?

Somehow in this process, the fate of thirty-nine Americans

came to be equated with that of a group of Shi'ite Moslems detained by Israeli troops during their occupation of Southern Lebanon. In an exclusive interview with hostages that was made possible by their captors, ABC reporter Charles Glass spoke with three hostages, including Allyn Conwell, an oil company salesman based in Oman. Conwell described the Israeli-held prisoners as "hostages" and expressed "profound sympathy" for the Amal cause.

Reporting on the Shi'ite Moslems on ABC's "World News Tonight," Don Kladstrup said that they are "the losers in life, the people who've been pushed from their homes in the South." A Shi'ite who said his two sons were in an Israeli prison told Kladstrup, "I sympathize with American families. My sons are hostages, too."

Television news reported the hijackers' demands not once, but frequently. If Israel would only release its Moslem detainees, then the hostages would go free. Through frequent repetition of that formula, the responsibility for the hostages was shifted from the hijackers and the Amal militia to Israel. To many viewers, Israel came to be seen as the jailer.

AT THE CENTER
OF THE UNIVERSE
In Beirut, the hijackers permitted interviews with their prisoners, and thus videotaped interviews themselves, distributing the footage freely to the world. The hijackers let reporters interview the pilot of Flight 847 in his cockpit while a terrorist held a gun to his head. If the United States attempted a rescue mission, said the pilot, "we'd all be dead men."

The story pushed other national concerns—the budget impasse, tax reform, the crisis in Central America—from the airwaves and the front pages, which is what the terrorists wanted. Because the story remained at the center of public attention, the pressures on the president were unrelenting, leaving him little space and time to maneuver.

From one quarter—the terrorists, the hostages, and their families—the president was pressured to negotiate. From another quarter, he was pressured to retaliate against the terrorists—perhaps, as the mayor of New York City suggested, by bombing Beirut International Airport. While some editorial writers praised the president for his restraint, others accused him of being "all talk, no action." A member of Congress branded him a "paper tiger."

The longer the crisis lasted, the greater the risk became for President Reagan. Similar pressures to do something— anything—had pushed President Carter into ordering a mission that ended in an aborted rescue attempt of the Iranian hostages. After ten days, people began comparing the crisis to the Iranian hostage crisis, and the president to his predecessor, Jimmy Carter.

In the meantime, by holding the world's attention for those seventeen days in June 1985, the terrorists reinforced their sense of self-importance and self-righteousness. At the end, they seemed reluctant to give up their hostages. "They were at the center of the universe," said ABC anchor Peter Jennings. "Why should they give them up?"

Yet, finally, the terrorists did release their hostages. And Israel, insisting that its action was unrelated to the crisis, released its Moslem detainees. Without any direct negotiations, the demands of the terrorists had been met. Regardless of how one felt about the outcome of the incident, no one could deny that it had been profoundly influenced by television. Even after the crisis had been resolved, familiar and perplexing questions still remained.

CRITICS AND DEFENDERS
Foremost among the critics of television was Prime Minister Margaret Thatcher of Great Britain. Thatcher said that news organizations should be urged to restrain their coverage. Somehow, she said, democracies must "find ways to starve the terrorist and the hijacker of the oxygen of publicity on which they depend."

U.S. Attorney General Edwin Meese III took Mrs. Thatcher's proposal a step further, saying that the White House might ask news organizations to adopt a voluntary code of restraint. Meese said that news organizations might be asked to accept "some principles reduced to writing." One principle could be the withholding of "interviews that might endanger the captives or endanger the successful conclusion of the incident."

[153]

Responding to Meese, John Corry wrote, "This is a terrible idea." Continuing, he asked:

How does one determine which interviews do the endangering? Is it more perilous, for instance, to interview a captive who apologizes for his captors, or a former Secretary of State who calls for a retaliatory strike? And, for that matter, who makes the determination? It is not realistic to expect competing news organizations to do it; it is chilling to think of the Government doing it for them. Either way, I think, Mr. Meese is onto a bad thing.

Not surprisingly, members of the television industry saw their role in the crisis as the proper one, and their influence, positive. In public assessments of their own performance, network executives, anchors, and correspondents could point to no serious shortcomings. "Was television manipulated?" NBC's John Chancellor asked rhetorically. "Yes," he answered, "by just about all the players in the game. Any free society can be manipulated."

ON BALANCE
Can television satisfy the public's desire—and right—to know without becoming a major actor in terrorist dramas or making bad situations worse? Should the government attempt to regulate the coverage of terrorist incidents? Zbigniew Brzezinski, who was President Carter's national security adviser, believes that television has one "potentially beneficial effect" on such a situation, and three negative effects.

"The only possible beneficial effect," according to Brzezinski, "is that, in the absence of any contact between the U.S. Government and the terrorists, television can fill a void that otherwise would have existed." The negative effects, says Brzezinski, are these:

First, television tends to transform what is essentially a political issue into a personal drama. It prevents the Government from dealing with the situation as a political problem and forces it to think of it as a personal problem.

[154]

Second, television becomes a medium for conveying the kidnappers' demands and for permitting them to appeal directly to the American people over the head of the Government for the acceptance of the demands. It thus enhances the bargaining capacity of the kidnappers.

And third, television humanizes the enemy, thereby also making it more difficult for the Government to respond firmly.

Brzezinski calls for "some mechanism for voluntary communication between Government and the media in these cases." Presumably, the government would be able to tell the networks when their restraint would be appreciated.

On balance, voluntary restraint seems to offer the best solution to what is clearly a conflict between the people's right to know and national security. Government controls would be bad for a number of reasons. First, if the media did not objectively, accurately, and credibly report terrorist acts, the public might lose confidence in both the press and the government. Second, attempts to impose media blackouts could easily lead terrorists to escalate the levels of violence to attract greater attention. Third, since a major goal of terrorists is to undermine authority and constitutional values, the limitation of free speech would be a victory for terrorism.

CHAPTER THIRTEEN

IS TERRORISM EVER JUSTIFIED?

*A few of the Jewish guerrillas who
blew up the King David Hotel in 1946
came back to the King David yesterday
evening—this time to sip champagne,
reminisce and mix their pride and
sorrow at the events of thirty-five
years ago. Even now, in middle age, they
had a stony toughness in their eyes.*

*The man who set the fuses was there.
The woman who made three futile telephone
calls of warning was there. The man who
brought the explosives into Jerusalem, the
man who guarded a key corridor, the man who
was drinking quietly in the bar, were there.
But their commander, Menachem Begin,
now Prime Minister of Israel, did not attend.
He had been invited and had apparently
vacillated all week, and finally did not appear.*

New York Times,
September 26, 1981

Among the former terrorists who observed the thirty-fifth anniversary of the bombing of the King David Hotel was Adina Hay-Nissan. In 1946, while still in her teens, she served as a courier for the Irgun. It was she who called in the warning, once the explosives had been planted. She recalls waiting for a long time outside the hotel for a signal that the charges had been set. Then she telephoned the hotel switchboard from a drugstore across the street. Speaking first in English, then in Hebrew, she said: "This is the Hebrew resistance uprising. We planted bombs in the hotel. Please vacate it immediately. See, we warned you."

Then she walked farther up Jaffa Road before telephoning the *Palestine Post* and the French Consulate, which was near the hotel. She continued walking, and as she passed the market at Mahane Yehuda, she recalls, "I heard the big explosion." When she later learned that the British had ignored her warnings, she said, "I was baffled; there we were, genuinely trying to save lives, and they took no heed."

The explosion took ninety-one lives—British, Jewish, and Arab. Israel Levi, the man who set the fuses, said at the reunion: "I was sorry for a long time afterwards, but they had a lot of time, more than a half an hour—they all had time to get out." What the terrorists did not know was that the hotel switchboard was not connected to the wing of the hotel in which the bomb had been planted—the wing occupied by the British—so the victims were not warned.

As the thirty-fifth reunion of the King David terrorists was under way, Teddy Kollek, the mayor of Jerusalem, arrived. In

1946, at the time of the bombing, he was a member of the moderate Jewish Agency, which deplored the Irgun's act as "dastardly" and described the group as "a gang of desperadoes." Grim-faced and in no mood for celebration, Mayor Kollek told the former members of the Irgun:

> I was then against terror, and I am today. . . . They were courageous groups, but their influence in getting the British out was limited. It's doubtful that we gained anything from acts of terror; perhaps more damage was done than anything else.

After the mayor had departed, he was denounced for his "collaboration with the British"—a charge that has also been leveled against Israel's first president, David Ben Gurion.

JUSTIFYING TERRORISM

The bitter charges that followed Teddy Kollek's appearance are understandable. Terrorists (and former terrorists) strive to justify their acts—just as we all strive to justify our behavior. The mayor had questioned both the justification and the accomplishments of the Irgun and of all terrorists.

One way in which the Irgun, the Official IRA, the Tupamaros, and other groups have justified their terrorism is by arguing that it can be selectively focused, harming only the "oppressors" and their property interests. The unexpected death toll in the King David bombing therefore deprived the Irgun of one of its justifications. More important, the death of innocents underscored the inherent weakness in the argument that terrorism can be selective. Terrorism is by its nature random and indiscriminate. This is partly the result of the destructive nature of such terrorist weapons as bombs and landmines. And it is partly the result of human nature—the caller is delayed, the line is busy, or the warning is dismissed as a crank call. Terrorists may take precautions to spare the innocent, but terrorism has a logic of its own. When elections fail, one turns to demonstrations; when those seem futile, empty buildings are blown up; when that tactic fails, kidnappings seem a logical next step. And then comes murder.

"LIBERATING VIOLENCE"

If the distinction between selective and random terrorism is a slippery justification, so, too, is the notion of "liberating violence," another widely used argument for terrorism. IRA terorrist Patrick Pearse, killed in the Easter Rising of 1916 wrote: "Bloodshed is a cleansing and sanctifying thing, and the nation which regards it as the final horror has lost its manhood." In the 1920s, the Italian fascist dictator Benito Mussolini spoke of the "'healthy effects of violence" on the personality. In the 1940s, Menachem Begin wrote: "A new generation grew up that knew no fear. We fight, therefore we are." And in the 1950s, Frantz Fanon applied the "liberating violence" argument to the anticolonial struggle, writing that "violence frees the colonized from their inferiority complex. It makes them fearless and restores their self-respect."

The argument that violence and terrorism can "liberate" the human personality is as dubious as the argument for "selective" terrorism. How has violence liberated the former terrorists of the King David incident who complain of guilt, misgivings, and sorrow? The notion of "liberating violence" reveals more about Pearse, Mussolini, Begin, Fanon, and its other proponents than it does about humankind in general. If violence liberates some, it does not liberate all. Martin Luther King, Jr., would later argue, and persuasively demonstrate, that the black person could "divest himself of passivity without arraying himself in vindictive force."

"NO ALTERNATIVE"

A third common justification for terrorism has been that there is simply no alternative. This was the argument of the People's Will. It is an argument that has been used by the Irgun, the IRA, the Weather Underground—in fact, by most terrorists. Some seem to stand on firmer ground than others. It is difficult to argue that there was "no alternative" to terrorism in Palestine, for the British were pledged to leave, and pledged to the creation of a Jewish state.

On the other hand, the British had vowed to remain in Ireland forever. The French had incorporated Algeria as a province of France. Perhaps for Irish and Algerian patriots, there was no alternative. As Sean MacBride explained his joining the IRA: "I was born into a situation in which violence predominated, and it seemed that the only way of getting rid of British rule, with all its injustices, was by means of a liberation movement." Perhaps there are situations in which violence is justified.

In a 1977 interview, MacBride expressed the "no-alternative-to-terrorism" argument more cautiously: "If injustice is so unbearable, so damaging, people probably have a right to react against it and defend themselves from it. If oppression amounts to genocide, for instance, people are entitled to fight back." Here perhaps is the strongest argument for terrorism that can be made and yet MacBride himself backs off, saying to the interviewer: "I think that if I were born again and were free to choose my own religion and philosophy, I would probably choose to be a Quaker, because Quakers are, I think, logical. They believe in pacifism and there is no equivocating about it."

GANDHI'S ALTERNATIVE
Mohandas K. Gandhi, often called "Mahatma," meaning "great soul," held no political office and led no guerrilla army or terrorist gang. Yet his thoughts and deeds mobilized millions of Indians, shook the British Empire, and challenged the most basic assumptions about politics and power. Gandhi pioneered a different kind of struggle from the violent struggles for which our century is noted, fatally undermining the argument that there is no alternative to violence.

Gandhi described terrorism as no more than "froth coming to the surface in an agitated liquid." In its place he proposed a strategy of nonviolent action that he called "Satyagraha," which can be translated as "truth force" or "firmness in a good cause." Gandhi describes Satyagraha as civil disobedience:

It is civil in the sense that it is not criminal. The lawbreaker . . . openly and civilly breaks [unjust laws], and quietly suffers the penalty for their breach. And in order to register his protest against the action of the law-givers, it is open to him to withdraw his cooperation from the State by disobeying such other laws whose breach does not constitute moral turpitude.

[162]

By resisting unjust laws in a nonviolent way, says Gandhi, resisters put themselves at risk, rather than their opponents. Thus they achieve a position that is morally superior to that of their enemies.

> I discussed in the earliest stages that pursuit of truth did not permit violence being inflicted on one's opponent, but that he must be weaned from error by patience and sympathy. For what appears to be truth to one may appear to be error to another. And patience means self-suffering. So the doctrine came to mean vindication of the truth—not by the infliction of suffering on the opponent, but on one's self.

Gandhi warned his followers—those who chose the path of civil disobedience—that Satyagraha was a life-or-death commitment: "We have had the courage to go to jail, to lose our homes and lands. Let us pray for the courage to go to the scaffold cheerfully or to become ashes in a consuming fire."

Beginning in the 1920s Gandhi skillfully orchestrated the first mass movement of nonviolent civil disobedience. Directed against British rule in India, Gandhi's strategy ultimately prevailed. Its success confirmed once more the truth of Terence MacSwiney's observation that those "who can endure the most" will triumph. But Gandhi's success also revealed the weakness of MacSwiney's position: endurance does not necessarily imply violence, as MacSwiney had assumed.

AMERICAN DISCIPLES

As Gandhi was achieving his greatest triumphs and worldwide prestige, a new generation of black leaders came of age in America, some of them disciples of Gandhi. Among these were James Farmer, who headed the Congress of Racial Equality (CORE), for twenty-four years, and the Reverend Martin Luther King, Jr., leader of the Southern Christian Leadership Conference, and winner of the 1964 Nobel Peace Prize.

The principles of nonviolent resistance preached and practiced by Dr. King, and by the American civil rights movement in general, owed much to the teachings of Gandhi. As King wrote in *Stride Toward Freedom*:

[163]

It was in this Gandhian emphasis on love and non-violence that I discovered the method for social reform that I had been seeking for so many months. The intellectual and moral satisfaction that I failed to gain from the utilitarianism of Bentham and Mill, the revolutionary methods of Marx and Lenin, the social contract theory of Hobbes, the "back-to-nature" optimism of Rousseau and the superhuman philosophy of Nietzsche, I found in the nonviolent resistance philosophy of Gandhi. I came to feel that this was the only morally and practically sound method open to oppressed people in their struggle for freedom.

Like Gandhi, King warned his followers that nonviolent civil disobedience could result in "martyrdom." But that was the very point of his and Gandhi's philosophy: to reveal the rightness and the truth of one's cause:

> The Negro was willing to risk martyrdom in order to move and stir the social conscience of his community and the nation. . . . He would force his oppressor to commit his brutality openly, with the rest of the world looking on. . . .

King emerged as a leader in the civil rights movement in 1955 after his victory in organizing a bus boycott in Montgomery, Alabama. By 1958 sympathy for the cause of civil rights led to nonviolent demonstrations in cities across the United States, resulting in the arrest of thousands of blacks and whites, and capturing the world's attention. In the 1960s, King's followers took over the sit-in technique that had been pioneered by James Farmer and CORE in the 1940s. Within one eighteen-month period, seventy thousand persons had taken part in sit-ins, and more than one hundred southern communities had desegregated one or more of their restaurants. At a momentous confrontation in Birmingham in 1963, politicians denied the demands of blacks for desegregation in public accommodations and equal opportunity in jobs. Police brutality provoked large and angry demonstrations as well as segregationist bombs. But in the end, white business leaders took effective power and forced an extremist mayor and police chief to yield to most of the demands.

Following the methods of nonviolent civil disobedience, Gandhi and his followers led India to independence. King and the civil rights movement achieved reforms and legislation that had been resisted for generations, convincing such powerful opponents as Senator Everett Dirksen of the rightness of their cause. Yielding to the objectives of the movement, Dirksen said, "There is no resisting the force of an idea whose time has come."

PRACTICAL
CONSIDERATIONS
Is terrorism ever morally justified? "Never!" say Gandhi and King. "Perhaps" and "sometimes," others say. But reviewing the history of terrorism, one might well ask, "Is terrorism justified on *practical* grounds?" Though terrorists have been successful in achieving such tactical objectives as gaining ransoms and freeing prisoners, they have rarely achieved their strategic objectives—revolution, for example. The only "successful" terrorists have been those who fought as part of a larger movement, such as a guerrilla campaign. No terrorists have achieved success that can be compared with that of Gandhi or King.

Moreover, as both Gandhi and King recognized, terrorism and other forms of violence are counterproductive. Gandhi warned that terrorism against the British would be "an easy, natural step to violence against our own people whom we consider to be an obstruction." And King warned: "If the Negro succumbs to the temptation of using violence in this struggle, unborn generations will be the recipients of a long and desolate night of bitterness." Those warnings have been confirmed in every society in which terrorism has been practiced, including our own.

In a letter to the supreme terrorist, Adolf Hitler, Mahatma Gandhi wrote:

You are leaving no legacy to your people of which they can be proud. They cannot take pride in a recital of cruel deeds, however skillfully planned.

[165]

This indeed is the legacy of terrorism, as it has been the subject of these chapters: "a recital of cruel deeds." In view of its dismal record, one wonders why terrorism persists, and what its attraction can be. The answer plainly lies in the deepest, darkest reaches of human nature. And so far, it is inaccessible to us.

FOR FURTHER READING

Alpert, Jane. *Growing Up Underground*. New York: Morrow, 1981. The memoirs of a former member of the Weather Underground Organization.

Baumann, Michael. *Terror or Love*. New York: Grove Press, 1979. The memoirs of a former member of the Baader-Meinhof gang.

Begin, Menachem. *The Revolt*. New York: Henry Schumer, 1951. A history of the Irgun told by its leader, who later became prime minister of Israel.

Bell, J. Bowyer. *The Secret Army: A History of the IRA*. Cambridge: MIT Press, 1974. The story of the Irish Republican Army and its splinter group, the Provisional IRA.

Branch, Taylor and Eugene M. Propper. *Labyrinth*. New York: Viking, 1982. The story of the assassination of Orlando Letelier, and of the investigation that proved the guilt of Chile's secret police.

Camus, Albert. *The Rebel*. New York: Knopf, 1954. A history of rebellion from the French Revolution to the mid-twentieth century.

Debray, Regis. *Revolution in the Revolution*. New York: Grove Press, 1967. A theory of revolutionary violence by a comrade of Che Guevara.

Dostoyevsky, Fyodor. *The Possessed.* New York: Random House, 1934. A novel based on the early conspiracies of Segey Nechaev and his circle.

Fanon, Frantz. *The Wretched of the Earth.* New York: Grove Press, 1965. An analysis of the impact of colonialism on the peoples of the Third World by a member of Algeria's National Liberation Front.

Frankfort, Ellen. *Kathy Boudin and the Dance of Death.* New York: Stein & Day, 1983. The story of one of the most notorious members of the Weather Underground organization.

Gandhi, Mohandas K. *Non-Violent Resistance.* New York: Schocken, 1961. The theory and practice of Gandhi's alternative to violence as set forth in his own words.

Jordan, David P. *The Revolutionary Career of Maximilien Robespierre.* New York: Free Press, 1985. A biography of the influential terrorist, based on his own writings and speeches.

Khaled, Leila. *My People Shall Live: The Autobiography of a Revolutionary.* London: Hodder and Stoughton, 1973. Memoirs of a noted terrorist of the Palestine Liberation Organization.

Khalidi, Rashid. *PLO Decision-Making During the 1982 War.* An account of why and how the PLO made the decisions it did during the fateful summer of 1982.

King, Martin Luther, Jr. *Stride Toward Freedom: The Montgomery Story.* New York: Harper & Row, 1958. How Gandhi's principles were successfully adapted and practiced by the civil rights movement led by Dr. King.

Koestler, Arthur. *Darkness at Noon.* New York: Bantam, 1966. A novel about communist political violence in Europe in the 1930s.

Laqueur, Walter. *Terrorism: A Study of National and International Political Violence.* Boston: Little, Brown, 1977. A comprehensive study of the roots of contemporary terrorism.

Laqueur, Walter, ed. *The Terrorism Reader: A Historical Anthology.* New York: New American Library, 1978. Readings on political violence from Aristotle to the IRA and the PLO.

Laqueur, Walter. *Germany Today: A Personal Report.* Boston: Little, Brown, 1985. An account of why young Germans have acted out their grievances "more violently than the rest."

Malraux, Andre. *Man's Fate.* New York: Vintage, 1969. A novel dealing with terrorism by Mao Zedong and the Chinese communists in the late 1920s.

Melman, Yossi. *The Master Terrorist: The True Story of Abu Nidal.* New York: Adama Books, 1986. This biography by an Israeli journalist makes a wealth of information on Abu Nidal available for the first time.

Netanyahu, Benjamin, ed. *Terrorism: How the West Can Win.* New York: Farrar, Straus & Giroux, 1986. Proposals for dealing with terrorism by a panel of thirty-eight international officials and experts who met in Washington in 1984.

Solzhenitsyn, Aleksandr. *Gulag Archipelago.* New York: Harper & Row, 1974. A novel about political violence in the Soviet system by a writer who was one of its victims.

Silone, Ignazio. *Bread and Wine.* New York: Signet, 1946. A novel about an attempted assassination of Benito Mussolini by Italian anarchists in the 1920s.

Taheri, Amir. *The Spirit of Allah.* New York: Adler & Adler, 1985. A biography of Ayatollah Ruhollah Khomeini, leader of Iran's fundamentalist revolution.

INDEX

Cagol, Margarita, 95–96
Carlos I of Portugal, 38
Carlos-the-Jackal, 123–127
Carnot, President, 38
Carter, Jimmy, 139
Castro, Fidel, 53, 126
*Catechism of the
  Revolutionary,* 31
Cells, 32
Central Intelligence Agency
  (CIA), 129
"Chicago eight," 77
Chile, 15
Civil war (Irish), 44
Cleaver, Eldridge, 33, 124
Colby, William, 129
Collins, Michael, 43, 44
Columbia University riots,
  53–54
Communism, 26
Congress of Racial Equality
  (CORE), 163
Cooperation among terrorists,
  127–128
Croatian separatists, 125
Cuba's support for terrorists,
  130
Curcio, Renato, 95–97

"Days of rage," 77
Delta Force, 139–140
Democratic Front for the
  Liberation of Palestine,
  113
De Valera, Eamon, 44
DINA, 15–16
Direct Action, 94–95, 98,
  125
Dohrn, Bernadine, 78–80,
  127

Dozier, James, 98–99
"Dynamiters," 41

Easter Rising of 1916, 42–43
"Ebony giant," 63
El Al, attacks on, 115–116
Elbrick, Charles, 64
Elizabeth (Empress) of
  Austria-Hungary, 37
Engels, Friedrich, 28, 55
Ensslin, Gudrun, 85–86, 93
Entebbe incident, 117, 141
Ewart-Biggs, Christopher,
  106

Faces of terrorism, 11–21
Falkland Islands, 70–71
FALN, 82
Fanon, Frantz, 58–59, 113,
  161
Farmer, James, 163–164
Fatah, 112–114, 118–119,
  127
FBI, 129
Fedayeen, 112
Fenian Brotherhood, 41
Ferdinand, Franz, 38
Fighters for the Freedom of
  Israel (LIEHI), 46–47
Fighting Communist Cells,
  125
Financing terrorism, 125–
  129
Forms of terrorism, 18–19
France's Front for the
  Liberation of Brittany, 124
Franco, Francisco, 56
Free Welsh Army, 124
French Enlightment, 25
French Revolution, 25

[172]